*I am privileged to write this book on different cuisines and for always being encouraged to follow my passion. With deep gratitude, I would like to thank my entire family, without whose support I would not have succeeded.*

*I am definitely living my dream and will continue on this journey.*

*I am grateful to all those helping hands, co-workers and friends who have helped me on my path.*

POONAM KAUR BINDRA

# Flavours From An
# Indian Rasoi

Popular Prakashan
www.popularprakashan.com

Published by Harsha Bhatkal
for Popular Prakashan Pvt. Ltd.
301, Mahalaxmi Chambers
22, Bhulabhai Desai Road
Mumbai 400026
www.popularprakashan.com


First Published 2021

ISBN: 978-81-948714-3-9



Food photography: Cartwork Imaging (Yogesh Tupe, Pankaj Dongre)
Poonam's photograph on the back cover: The Open Window (Pankaj Gahiwad)
Design: Anjali Sawant

Printed by
Saurabh Printers (P) Ltd.
Plot No. 67 A-68, Ecotech, Ext. I
Kasna, Greater Noida-201306 (U.P)

# AUTHOR'S NOTE

*Cookery is a wholly unselfish art: All good cooks, like great artists, must have an audience worth cooking for.*

— ***Andre Simon***

I was always in a relationship with food. They say if one has a passion for cooking it eventually pays off. Being a creative person all my life, especially when it comes to cooking, I became my own type of chef. We all know cooking is love made visible and that food tastes better when you eat it with someone you love. I was born in Nashik to parents who were passionate about good food. My father loved cutting out the most amazing recipes from newspapers and enhancing his scrap book in his free time and my mother used to dish out the most amazing recipes- this was my early introduction to food at a very tender age.

My passion was further driven when I got married into a joint family in Aurangabad, all of whom were food critics, hence my cooking was actually the result of my family's insatiable appetite. No one realised it was different than planned, but it turned out great. It's all about having an open mind and being creative.

Proceeding ahead with my maxim, I created my own Facebook page called Art of Cooking which has more than 1,00,000 followers and started posting my home made recipes there. Then I started my Youtube channel which received tremendous support from the viewers. Nonetheless, I found a bigger platform by printing a new recipe every weekend in the newspaper, Lokmat Times and sharing my ideas with society. Then came some magazines where I got an opportunity to write and the journey is still ongoing. The main force behind my success is my husband Ravinder Singh Bindra and my devoted son Amandeep Singh Bindra.

# CONTENTS

## MAHARASHTRIAN FLAVOURS



## BENGALI FLAVOURS



## SOUTHERN FLAVOURS

# NORTHERN Flavours

# Karah Parshad

INGREDIENTS

| | |
|---|---|
| 1 cup ghee | 2 cups water |
| 1 cup wholewheat flour | 1 cup sugar |

METHOD

- In a kadai, add the ghee on low heat.
- Gently, add in the flour and stir continuously for approximately 15 minutes, till brown.
- In other pan, boil the water, add the sugar and stir till it dissolves.
- Add the sugar syrup to the flour and whisk briskly to avoid lumps.
- Cook till the ghee separates from the mixture and take off the heat.
- Serve hot.

*Serves 4*

Note: Try using flour that is a bit grainy and coarse for the perfect texture.

# Nadru Kebab

## INGREDIENTS

- 6 pieces lotus stem (nadru)
- 1¼ teaspoons teaspoon salt + as required
- 2 medium potatoes, boiled, peeled, and roughly chopped
- 6 green chillies, chopped
- 4 teaspoons chopped ginger
- 2½ tablespoons chopped coriander leaves
- 2 tablespoons yellow chilli powder
- 1 tablespoon garam masala powder
- A pinch of cardamom powder
- A pinch of nutmeg powder
- 2 tablespoons breadcrumbs
- Oil for deep-frying

## METHOD

- Scrape the lotus stems thoroughly under running water as it has a lot of mud on it. Peel and slice thinly.
- Boil the lotus stems in water with a little salt till tender. Drain and set aside to cool.
- Place the lotus stem in a food processor and grind to a fine paste.
- Add the potatoes, green chillies, ginger and coriander leaves and grind well.
- Add the salt, all the spice powders, and breadcrumbs and grind to make a smooth dough. Moisten your palms and shape the dough into flat, round kebabs.
- Heat the oil in a pan and deep-fry the kebabs into batches on moderate heat, till golden brown.
- Serve hot with green chutney.

*Serves 4*

Note: This tasty evening snack/starter is very healthy for adolescent girls and has been proven to be helpful for growing children, menopausal women, elderly suffering from osteoporosis, anaemia, or other bone problems.

# Shalgam Kebab

## INGREDIENTS

- ¼ cup skinless split Bengal gram (chana dal), soaked overnight
- 2 dried red chillies
- 3 medium turnips (shalgam), peeled and cut into quarters
- 1 potato, peeled, boiled and mashed
- 1 tablespoon dried pomegranate seed powder
- 1 tablespoon roasted cumin powder
- 1 teaspoon coriander powder
- ¾ teaspoon garam masala
- Salt to taste
- ½ teaspoon lemon juice
- 2-3 teaspoons spring onion with greens, finely chopped
- 1 green chilli, finely chopped
- Handful of coriander leaves, finely chopped
- 10 mint leaves, chopped
- ½ cup oil
- 3 tablespoons corn flour
- 1 egg, beaten (optional)

## METHOD

- Boil the soaked split Bengal gram with the chillies for 15-20 minutes, or until dry and cooked. Drain and set aside.
- Add ½ cup of water to a pan. Add the turnips and cover and cook for 25 minutes or till the turnips are tender. If needed, you can add more water.
- Mash the turnips and place in a muslin cloth. Squeeze out the excess liquid to make it dry.
- Place in a bowl, add the mashed potatoes, and cooked gram with all the remaining ingredients except the oil, corn flour and egg. Mix and knead together till well combined.
- Shape the dough into patties. Spread the corn flour in a plate. In another plate, break the egg and season with salt. Dip the patty in the corn flour and then in the egg.
- Heat the oil in a kadai and deep-fry the kebabs on low heat till medium brown on both the sides. Serve hot with chutney and lemon wedges.

*Serves 4*

---

Note: With a vegetarian/non-vegetarian option this recipe provides a twist to the otherwise boring turnip.

# Karachi Wadiyan

## INGREDIENTS

| For the wadis | For the stock |
|---|---|
| 3 cups wholewheat flour | 1 inch ginger, crushed |
| Salt to taste | A few black peppercorns |
| 5-6 slightly crushed black peppercorns | 1-2 green chillies |
| A pinch of asafoetida | 1-2 cloves |
| ½ teaspoon red chilli powder | ½ inch cinnamon |
| ¼ teaspoon cumin powder | 1 carrot |
| A pinch of soda bicarbonate (optional) | 8-10 French beans |
| Oil for deep-frying | 4-6 spinach leaves |
| | Salt to taste |
| | 2 cups water |

## METHOD

- Knead together the flour, salt and water as required to make a stiff dough. Let the dough rest for 1 hour.
- Place the dough in a tub with water and leave it untouched for 15 minutes. The water will become white. Change the water and flip the dough again, and leave it in the water.
- Gently knead the dough in the water, drain the water.
- Repeat the process till the water no more turns white while washing it. This process makes the dough gluten free.
- Squeeze out the gluten from the dough and discard it. Add the spices to the dough.
- Take small portions of the dough and shape them into small balls.
- Take a pan or steamer and add enough water to poach the dough balls.
- Add the stock ingredients to the water. Let the stock boil for a few minutes and then drop the wadis into it.

- When the wadis start to float, lower the heat and let them cook till they become fluffy. Drain and cool the wadis.
- Heat the oil in pan, and deep-fry the wadis till golden brown. Use them in pulav or curries.

*Serves 4*

---

Tip: You can also sun-dry these wadis and store them for later use.

Note: This is a very handy recipe which can be prepared and stored beforehand making cooking quick and easy. It is loved by the elders of the house because it's traditional and it suits young working women too because it's quick to prepare. I learnt how to make Karachi Wadiyan, Peshawari Chicken and Lahori Murg Cholay from my Dadi (grandmother) who moved from Peshawar to Bombay, during the Partition.

# Kashmiri Saag

## INGREDIENTS

| | |
|---|---|
| 4 tablespoons mustard oil | 25 garlic cloves |
| 3 black cardamoms | 2 bunch spinach leaves |
| 10 Kashmiri whole red chillies | Salt to taste |

## METHOD

- Heat the mustard oil in a pressure cooker till the oil begins to emit smoke.
- Switch off the heat and allow the oil to cool a little. Then heat the oil again and add the cardamoms, Kashmiri whole red chillies, garlic cloves, spinach leaves, a little water and salt.
- Cook in a pressure cooker till the pressure is released once (1 whistle).
- Open the lid and mix well. Cook covered on low heat for 15 minutes. Serve hot.

*Serves 4*

---

Note: Kashmiri saag is not only a recipe to relish in the winters as it is packed with everything your body requires then, but also an easy to make, low calories, full of nutrients vegetable that must be eaten at least once a week, not just by the elderly, but also by children and especially expectant mothers.

# Amritsari Kulcha Cholay

## INGREDIENTS

### For the kulchas

3 cups refined flour

Salt to taste

2 tablespoons yogurt

½ cup milk

1 teaspoons sugar

2 teaspoons desi ghee

### For the stuffing

1 medium onion, chopped

2 medium potatoes, boiled and grated

1 green chilli, chopped finely

1 teaspoon red chilli powder

1 teaspoon dried pomegranate seed powder

1 tablespoon roasted cumin powder

1 inch ginger, chopped

1 teaspoon coriander powder

1 teaspoon garam masala

2 tablespoons coriander leaves

5 tablespoons butter

### For the cholay

2 cups chickpeas (Kabuli chana), soaked overnight and boiled

½ teaspoon cooking soda

2 tablespoons coriander leaves

### For the masala

12 black peppercorns

1 black cardamom

6 cloves

1 inch cinnamon

1½ teaspoons red chilli powder

1 teaspoon cumin powder

2 teaspoons coriander powder

1 tablespoon ghee

1 teaspoon dried pomegranate seed powder

1 teaspoon dried mango powder

Salt to taste

### For the chutney

75 grams tamarind, soaked in warm water for ½ an hour

1 teaspoon red chilli powder

2-3 green chillies, roughly chopped

1 bunch mint leaves, broken with hands

1 big potato, boiled, peeled and diced

1 medium onion, finely chopped

Salt to taste

2 tablespoons tamarind water

## METHOD

### For the kulchas

- Sieve the flour. Add the salt, yogurt, milk, sugar, ghee and 1 cup of water and knead together to make a soft dough. Place it under a wet cloth for an hour. This will ferment the dough to make soft kulchas.
- For the stuffing, mix together the onion, potatoes, salt, green chilli, red chilli powder, pomegranate seed powder, cumin powder, ginger powder, coriander powder, garam masala powder and coriander leaves.
- Take a piece of dough and flatten it with your palms. Place some of the above mixture on the flattened dough and seal it from the centre. Flatten with your palms again.
- Dust some flour on the kulcha and roll gently as it might open in between.
- Apply water on one side of the kulcha and place it in a hot tandoor with the wet side touching the tandoor.
- Cook till crisp. Remove it carefully.
- Apply butter and crush kulcha between your palms. Serve hot.

### For the cholay

- To the chickpeas, add the cooking soda and water to cover and place the utensil on heat.
- Pound the whole spices together.
- Add the pounded masala, red chilli powder, cumin powder and coriander powder. Boil for 10 minutes.
- Add the ghee, pomegranate powder, dried mango powder and salt. Stir and cook for another 10 minutes. Garnish with coriander leaves.

### For the chutney

- Mix all the ingredients together and serve with cholay.

*Serves 4*

# Lyadir Tczhaman

## INGREDIENTS

- 1 teaspoon mustard oil
- 1 teaspoon asafoetida
- 1 teaspoon dried ginger powder
- 1 teaspoon fennel powder
- ½ teaspoon turmeric powder
- 2 Kashmiri red chillies
- ½ cup whisked yogurt
- 150 grams cottage cheese, cubed
- ½ cup heavy cream
- 1 teaspoon black pepper powder
- Salt to taste

## METHOD

- Heat the oil, add the asafoetida, ginger powder, fennel powder, turmeric powder and red chillies. Fry for a few seconds, and then add the yogurt and cottage cheese.
- Whisk the mixture continuously to avoid curdling. Once it comes to a boil, add the cream. Cook on low heat for 10 minutes. You can add a little water to adjust the consistency.
- Add the pepper powder and salt. Serve.

*Serves 4*

---

Note: This is a Kashmiri cottage cheese dish which is easy to prepare, easy to digest, and has a delicate flavour. A thicker consistency of this gravy makes a perfect filling for rolls, or with rice in a tiffin box.

# Peshawari Chicken

INGREDIENTS

- 3 tablespoons oil or ghee
- 1 bay leaf
- 4-5 cardamoms
- 1 inch cinnamon
- 4-5 cloves
- 1 cup onions, chopped
- 2 tablespoons ginger- garlic paste
- ½ cup tomatoes, chopped
- 1 teaspoon cashew nut paste
- 1 kg chicken, curry cut pieces
- 1 teaspoon garam masala powder
- 1 teaspoon turmeric powder
- 1 teaspoon cumin powder
- 1 teaspoon coriander powder
- ½ teaspoon red chilli powder
- Salt to taste
- 3 tablespoons yogurt
- 1 tablespoon gram flour
- A pinch of saffron mixed in 1 teaspoon water
- 1 teaspoon chopped coriander leaves

METHOD

- Heat the oil or ghee in a pan or kadai. Add the bay leaf, cardamoms, cinnamon and cloves.
- Stir for few seconds and then add the chopped onions and ginger-garlic paste. Cook on medium heat till the onion turns light brown. Add the chopped tomato and cashew nut paste. Cook for 2 minutes.
- Add the chicken pieces and cook on low heat for 10 minutes, stirring at regular intervals for even cooking.
- Add the garam masala, turmeric powder, cumin powder, coriander powder and red chilli powder, stir and add the salt. Add 1 cup of water and cook for 2 minutes.
- Mix the yogurt, gram flour and saffron water in a bowl. Add this mixture to the chicken. Cook for 5 minutes or till the chicken is well cooked and tender.
- Garnish with chopped coriander leaves and serve with rice or roti.

*Serves 4*

---

Note: Adding protein to our diets with great flavour has become so easy with recipes like this one. Whether you're serving guests or family members, this dish brings smiles at the dinner table.

# Lahori Murg Cholay

## INGREDIENTS

- 4 tablespoons butter
- 1 chicken, cut into 12 pieces
- 1 cup chickpeas
- 1 inch cinnamon
- 12 black peppercorns
- 8-10 green cardamoms
- 10 cloves
- 1 teaspoon tea powder
- 2 tablespoons ghee
- 5 medium onions, sliced
- 1 inch ginger, finely chopped
- 10 garlic cloves, finely chopped
- 1 cup tomato purée
- 1½ teaspoons dried pomegranate seed powder
- 1½ teaspoons red chilli powder
- 2 tablespoons coriander powder
- 1 teaspoon cumin powder
- ½ teaspoon turmeric powder
- Salt to taste
- 1 teaspoon garam masala
- A few coriander leaves

## METHOD

- Heat the butter in a pan and fry the chicken for 5 minutes until it turns white. Remove and set aside.
- Soak the chickpeas overnight or at least for 6 hours. Make a potli (small bag) with a piece of muslin cloth consisting of the cinnamon, peppercorns, cardamoms, cloves and tea powder.
- In a pressure cooker, add the chickpeas, potli and salt and pressure cook for 30 minutes or till done.
- Heat the ghee in a kadai, and fry the sliced onions till light brown. Add the ginger, garlic cloves and fry for a minute.
- Add the tomato purée, pomegranate seed powder, red chilli powder, coriander powder, cumin powder, turmeric powder, salt to taste and mix well. Add the chicken, chickpeas, salt and 2 cups of water and cook covered. Cook till the chicken is done. This will take almost 25 minutes on medium heat and then take out the potli.
- Add the garam masala and coriander leaves and stir for a minute. Serve hot.

*Serves 6*

# Tabakh Maaz

## INGREDIENTS

| | |
|---|---|
| 500 grams mutton, preferably ribs | 1 bay leaf |
| 2 cups milk | 1 teaspoon cumin seeds |
| 1 tablespoon fennel seeds | 1 teaspoon turmeric powder |
| 1 inch cinnamon | 1 teaspoon red chilli powder |
| 5-6 cardamoms | Salt to taste |
| ½ teaspoon dry ginger | ¼ cup ghee |

## METHOD

- Add all the ingredients together in a pan except the ghee, and cook covered for 2 hours on low heat.
- Stir occasionally to prevent it from sticking at the bottom of the pan. The milk will reduce during this process.
- Uncover the pan and continue to cook on high heat till the milk dries up completely.
- Heat the ghee in a separate pan, add it to the mutton ribs and fry till they are brown on both the sides. Serve hot.

*Serves 4*

Note: This is a Kashmiri Style Mutton Ribs dish.

# Kunna Gosht

INGREDIENTS

500 grams mutton leg
4-5 tablespoons ghee
1 medium onion, ground to a paste
1 teaspoon ginger paste
1 teaspoon garlic paste
1 teaspoon red chilli powder
½ teaspoon turmeric powder
1 tablespoon yogurt
2 cups mutton stock
1½ tablespoons wholewheat flour
Sliced ginger, for garnishing
Chopped coriander, for garnishing
2 green chillies cut lengthwise, for garnishing

For the spice mix

2 whole cloves
½ tablespoon cumin seeds
½ tablespoon coriander seeds
½ tablespoon black peppercorns
A pinch of mace
A pinch of rock salt

## METHOD

- Wash the mutton leg and trim off the excess fat. Cut into large pieces and set aside.
- Grind together all the spice mix ingredients to make a powder. Set aside. (You can also roast the whole spices first and then grind them for more flavour.)
- Heat the ghee in a large pan, add the mutton and sear it until it has browned all over. Remove and set aside.
- In the same pan, add the onions and cook till brown. Add the ginger paste, garlic paste, red chilli powder, turmeric powder and blend together.
- Add the spice mix powder and yogurt and whisk the mixture to prevent it from curdling. Add the meat and cook covered on low heat till it done. It takes approximately 40 minutes. Keep stirring at intervals.
- Make a slurry with water and flour and add to the meat towards the end. Bring to a boil and cook for a couple of minutes. The gravy needs to be thick.
- Garnish with sliced ginger, coriander, and green chillies. Serve hot with naan.

*Serves 4*

---

Note: Kunna means mitti ka bartan or earthen pot, broad from the base and narrow on top. This recipe came from the nomads. This is quite similar to Nehari but it originates from the region of Chiniot, in Punjab (Peshawar) which is also famous for its carved wooden furniture.

This recipe helps with muscle growth in young boys and girls, athletes and fitness enthusiasts, as well as individuals recovering from injuries, due to the high protein content in mutton. Apart from that, who wouldn't love to come home to this tasty mutton dish after a long day at work. This is a thick gravy to be relished with naan.

# Kashmiri Kahwa

INGREDIENTS

1 inch cinnamon

2 cardamoms

1 pinch saffron strands

A few dry rose petals

Sugar or honey to taste

1 bag green tea bag (Kashmiri green tea if available)

Sliced almonds, for garnishing

Chopped walnuts, for garnishing

METHOD

- In a saucepan, add 2 cup of water and all the other ingredients except the green tea bag. Bring to boil on high heat for 3-4 minutes.
- Add the green tea bag and boil for another 2 minutes. Strain and serve with sliced almonds, chopped walnuts.
- If you are using honey as sweetener, adjust the sweetness before serving.

*Serves 4*

Note: Apart from being helpful for viral flu, cold and cough, this kahwa makes for a refreshing beverage after a long hectic day. During the monsoon, on winter evenings, or even on dates—if you want to avoid your regular tea, what other healthier option could there be?

# Gur ka Halwa

## INGREDIENTS

1 cup ghee

1 cup semolina (sooji/rawa)

1 cup jaggery, crushed and soaked in water for 15 minutes

½ cup milk

1 tablespoon melon seeds

¼ cup fried cashew nuts, lightly crushed

A pinch of orange food colouring (optional)

## METHOD

- Heat the ghee in a kadai and fry the semolina on low heat till it turns light brown.
- Add the soaked jaggery and fry for 15 minutes.
- Add the milk slowly and as per your taste. Cook till the milk evaporates.
- Add the melon seeds and cashew nuts. Add the orange colouring if needed.
- Serve hot.

*Serves 4*

---

Note: Gur ka halwa is made in Punjab and consumed during winters as it provides warmth and strength to the body.

This is a simple yet beautiful and mouth-watering dessert. It is also perfect for warding off a cough and cold.

# Pinni

## INGREDIENTS

1½ cups split black gram (urad dal)

2 cups pure ghee

2 cups wholewheat flour, sieved

½ cup edible gum (gond), ground and sieved

1½ cups mixed dried fruits, finely chopped (almonds, pistachio, raisins)

1 tablespoon dried ginger powder (saunth)

1 teaspoon black pepper powder (optional)

1½ cups ground sugar, sieved

## METHOD

- For the black gram flour, wipe the black gram and place in sunlight for 2 hours. Dry-roast and grind to a flour. Sieve and use.
- In a kadai, add 1 cup of ghee and the wholewheat flour and cook on low heat till brown. Do not increase the heat or the flour will stick to the bottom. Cook till golden.
- In another pan, add the remaining ghee and roast the black gram flour on low heat till brown.
- Add the gond to either of the flours and cook on high heat for 5 minutes till the gond fluffs up like popcorn. Take off the heat, add the ginger powder and pepper powder and mix.
- Mix both the flour in one vessel.
- Add the dried fruits and cook. Once it comes to room temperature, add the sugar powder and check the sweetness and adjust if necessary. Mix well.
- Shape the mixture into cylindrical shaped pinni.
- Store in an airtight container.

*Serves 4*

---

Note: Pinni is a must have in every Punjabi house where a baby is born. For generations, pinni is known to be a staple for new mothers, helping them recover from the stresses and strains of child birth. The elderly also enjoy pinni after their meals, especially during winters.

This recipe is very dear to our family as it has been made the same way for generations during the winter season. It's a must during the winters in every Punjabi family.

# NAWABI Flavours

# Paneer Golconda

## INGREDIENTS

500 grams cottage cheese (paneer), cut into 2-inch cubes

1 teaspoon green chilli paste

1 teaspoon ginger-garlic paste

1 teaspoon lemon juice

1 teaspoon garam masala powder

½ cup fresh coriander leaves

½ cup hung yogurt

Salt to taste

Butter, for brushing on top

Cream, for serving

## METHOD

- Marinate the cottage cheese cubes with the green chilli paste, ginger-garlic paste, lemon juice, garam masala powder, fresh coriander leaves, hung yogurt and salt.
- Place the marinated cottage cheese cubes on skewers and cook in a clay oven.
- Brush with butter and serve with fresh cream.

*Serves 4*

---

Note: This is a royal dish from the kingdom of Golconda. It's served with mint chutney for a delectable flavour.

# Soya Shikampuri Kebab

## INGREDIENTS

250 grams soya granules, soaked overnight

¼ teaspoon turmeric powder

1 tablespoon red chilli powder

2-3 green chillies, chopped

2 tablespoons fresh coriander leaves, chopped

1 tablespoon mint leaves, chopped

1 teaspoon lemon juice

Salt to taste

4-5 tablespoons roasted gram flour

Oil for deep-frying

Chaat masala, for garnishing

**For the stuffing**

⅙ cup hung yogurt

1 medium onion, cut into small pieces

1 green chilli, cut into small pieces

## METHOD

- Mix together all the stuffing ingredients in a bowl and set aside.
- Drain the soya granules and remove the excess water.
- In a pan, add the soya granules, turmeric powder, red chilli powder, green chillies, coriander leaves and mint leaves. Cook till the water evaporates. Cool and grind to a fine paste. Add to the paste, lemon juice and salt to the gram flour and mix well.
- Take a portion of the mixture and flatten it with your palms to form a kebab. Place ½ teaspoon stuffing in the centre, cover from all sides till closed and flatten it.
- Deep-fry the kebabs till brown.
- Sprinkle some chaat masala and served with mint chutney.

*Serves 4*

# Kathal ki Shammi

### INGREDIENTS

- 1 kg jackfruit (kathal), cut into small pieces and peeled
- 1 cup skinless split Bengal gram (chana dal), soaked for 20 minutes
- ½ teaspoon yellow chilli powder or red chilli powder
- 1 teaspoon cumin seeds
- 6 cloves
- 6 black peppercorns
- 2 black cardamoms
- 1 bay leaf
- 1 teaspoon ginger paste
- 1 teaspoon garlic paste
- 2 green chillies
- 1 teaspoon coriander leaves, chopped
- 1 onion, chopped
- Salt to taste
- Oil or ghee for shallow-frying

### METHOD

- In a deep utensil, add the jackfruit, split Bengal gram and 3 cups of water, and bring to a boil.
- Add the yellow chilli powder, cumin seeds, cloves, black peppercorns, cardamoms, bay leaf, ginger paste, garlic paste and chillies. Cook till soft. Set aside to cool. Remove the bay leaf.
- Grind the mixture to a thick paste.
- Add the chopped coriander, onion and salt to the paste. Mix.
- Shape the paste into small round cakes or shammis with your hands.
- Heat the oil in a pan and shallow-fry the shammis till golden brown.
- Serve hot with green chutney.

*Serves 4*

---

Tip: To make yellow chilli powder, remove the seeds of dry whole red chillies and grind to a powder.

# Gobi Mussallam

INGREDIENTS

- 1 medium cauliflower
- 1 large onion, finely sliced
- ½ cup ghee
- ½ cup yogurt
- 1 teaspoon ginger
- 1 blade mace
- 1 inch cinnamon
- 5 green cardamoms
- 5 cloves
- 1 tablespoon poppy seeds
- 5 cashew nuts
- ¼ teaspoon turmeric powder
- ¼ teaspoon red chilli powder
- Salt to taste
- ⅓ cup green peas
- ¼ teaspoon cumin seeds

METHOD

- Wash the cauliflower, cut off the main stock, and remove the leaves.
- Fry the onion in ghee till golden brown and grind to a paste using 1 tablespoon yogurt. Separately grind the ginger, mace, cinnamon, cardamoms and cloves.
- Lightly roast the poppy seeds and cashew nuts on a griddle and grind to a paste.
- Par-boil the cauliflower in half a litre of salted water and remove.
- Heat the ghee in the kadai in which the onion was fried and place the cauliflower upside down so that it turns light brown. Then turn and cook the stem portion for some time. Remove and place in the yogurt. Mix together all the ground ingredients, chilli powder, turmeric powder and salt and sprinkle it over the cauliflower.
- In a flat vessel, place the cauliflower along with the marinade. Pour the remaining ghee from the kadai, over the top and sides; saving 1 tablespoon for the peas.
- Cover and place slow charcoal fire on the lid and also below the vessel. Cook till the masala is dry but moist and the cauliflower is dry. Meanwhile, in the kadai, heat a tablespoon of ghee and add the cumin seeds, when they begin to crackle add the green peas, a pinch of salt and cook till tender. When the cauliflower is done serve on a bed of peas.

*Serves 4*

# Kakori Kebab

## INGREDIENTS

4 cups mutton mince
1 cup chickpeas (Kabuli chana), boiled
1 cup onion, chopped
6 green chillies
½ cup raw papaya paste
10-14 cashew nuts, roasted
2 tablespoons musk melon seeds (magaz)
½ cup mutton fat
Salt to taste
2 eggs
2 tablespoons coriander leaves, chopped
3 tablespoons butter/ghee
1 tablespoon kewra water

For the kakori masala

6 black peppercorns
8 green cardamoms
2 black cardamoms
½ teaspoon mace
1 teaspoon nutmeg
4 cloves
2 tablespoons cumin seeds
10 whole dry red chillies
1 inch cinnamon

## METHOD

- Dry-roast all the kakori masala ingredients till fragrant. Cool and grind the mixture to a fine powder.
- To the mince add the chickpeas, onion, chillies, raw papaya paste, cashew nuts, musk melon seeds, mutton fat, salt, eggs and coriander. Grind together to a fine paste.
- To the mince paste, add the ghee and mix well. Add 1 tablespoon kakori masala and kewra water and mix well. Place the mixture in the freezer for 30 minutes. This will make it easy to handle the paste. Divide the mince into equal portions and wrap it around kebab skewers.
- Cook on charcoal till golden brown. Remove the kebabs from skewers and serve hot with chutney, onion rings and lime wedges.

*Serves 6*

Note: Kakori kebabs were originally created for people with dental issues since these kebabs tend to be super soft and chewy.

# Galouti ke Kebab

## INGREDIENTS

1½ kg leg of lamb or mutton, boneless

250 grams lamb fat

Ghee for frying + as required

**For the first marinade**

1 teaspoon ginger-garlic paste

¼ cup raw papaya paste

¼ cup onions, sliced and browned

½ teaspoon red chilli powder

1 tablespoon roasted cashew nut powder

2 tablespoons coriander stem, finely chopped

3 tablespoons fresh cream

Salt to taste

**For the second marinade**

½ teaspoon cinnamon powder

A pinch of clove powder

1 teaspoon potli masala powder

½ teaspoon garam masala powder

½ teaspoon black pepper powder

½ teaspoon black cardamom powder

½ teaspoon onion powder

½ teaspoon mace and green cardamom powder

½ teaspoon caraway seed (shahi jeera) powder

A pinch of nutmeg powder

3 teaspoons roasted gram flour

A drop of kewra water/ittar

2 teaspoons saffron water

## METHOD

- Mince together the leg of lamb and the lamb fat to a very fine paste.
- For the first marinade, add the ginger-garlic paste, raw papaya paste, browned onions, red chilli powder, cashew nut powder, coriander stem, fresh cream and salt to the mince.
- The most important part of making galouti is mixing and kneading the mince well. Add a little ghee while kneading, if required. Set aside for 2 hours.
- Add all the ingredients of the second marinade to the mince. Mix well and knead till soft. Add more ghee if needed. Make a well in the centre of the mince and place a bowl containing a piece of burning charcoal. Sprinkle clove powder followed by a little ghee on the charcoal. Cover the utensil with a tight lid and smoke the mince.
- Remove the charcoal after 10 minutes and mix the mince well. Make small galouti (patties) of the mince. Heat the ghee on a tawa and fry the galouti on medium heat, on both sides till done.

*Serves 4*

---

Note: There is no particular shape of this kebab, the mince is simply taken in one's hand and thrown into the griddle.

# Chicken Noorjahani

## INGREDIENTS

- 1 kg chicken
- 2 cups yogurt, whipped
- 6 teaspoons ghee
- 3 bay leaves
- 2 onions, finely chopped
- ½ cup milk
- A pinch of saffron strands
- 5-6 roasted sultanas, for garnishing
- 5-6 roasted almonds, for garnishing

**For the paste**

- 4 green chillies
- 1 teaspoon aniseed
- ½ inch ginger
- 8 garlic cloves
- 3 brown cardamoms
- 4-5 cloves
- 1 inch cinnamon
- 1 teaspoon salt

## METHOD

- For the paste, grind together the green chillies, aniseed, ginger, garlic, cardamoms, cloves, cinnamon and salt with a little water.
- Add the paste to the chicken and prick the meat for the flavour to soak in.
- Add the whipped yogurt to the chicken and set aside to marinate for a minimum of 3 hours.
- Heat the ghee in a pan, add the bay leaves and onions and sauté on high heat till golden brown.
- In another pan, warm the milk, add the saffron, stir gently and set aside.
- Add the marinated chicken to the sautéed onions. Let it cook on high heat for 5-6 minutes.
- Pour the milk into the chicken and cook on low heat for 30-40 minutes.
- Garnish with the roasted sultanas and almonds. Serve hot.

*Serves 4*

# Maash ki Dal

## INGREDIENTS

1 cup skinless split black gram (urad dal)
5 tablespoons oil
5 garlic cloves, minced
1 inch ginger, minced
1 medium onion
2 small tomatoes, chopped
½ teaspoon red chilli powder
1½ teaspoons coriander powder
1½ teaspoons cumin powder
¼ teaspoon turmeric powder
1 teaspoon cumin seeds
Salt to taste
Fresh coriander leaves, for garnishing
Green chillies, for garnishing
Ghee or butter, for garnishing

## METHOD

- Wash the split black gram and soak for 1 hour.
- Heat the oil in a pan, add the garlic, ginger and onion. Sauté till brown and add this mixture to the chopped tomatoes, chilli powder, coriander powder, cumin powder, turmeric powder, cumin seeds and continue cooking till the oil rises to the surface and the tomatoes are soft.
- Add the split black gram along with 2 cups of water and salt. Bring to a boil and cook covered on low heat till the dal is cooked. Take off the lid and continue to cook on high heat to dry out the excess water from the dal. Adjust the seasoning.
- Garnish with chopped coriander, green chilli and a dash of butter or ghee.

*Serves 4*

# Hyderabadi Khatti Dal

## INGREDIENTS

- 1 cup skinless split red lentils (masoor dal)
- 1 cup split pigeon peas (toor dal)
- 1 tablespoon ginger-garlic paste
- ½ teaspoon turmeric powder
- 1 tablespoon red chilli powder
- 2 medium tomatoes, chopped
- 2 springs curry leaves
- ¾ cup tamarind water
- 2 green chillies, sliced
- 2 sprigs coriander leaves
- Salt to taste

**For the tempering**

- ½ cup oil
- 2 tablespoons ghee
- 6 whole red chillies
- 6 garlic cloves
- 1 sprig curry leaves

## METHOD

- Clean and wash the split red lentils and split pigeon peas and soak for 30 minutes.
- In a pressure cooker, add the dals, ginger-garlic paste, turmeric powder, red chilli powder, tomatoes, curry leaves and 3 cups of water. Cook till the pressure is released once (1 whistle). Lower the heat and cook for 10 minutes. The dal has to be soft.
- Mash the cooked dal in the cooker with the back of the ladle to fine paste. Add the tamarind water, green chillies, coriander leaves and salt. Cook covered on low heat for another 10-15 minutes.
- For the tempering, heat the oil in a pan and add a little ghee to it. Add the red chillies, garlic and curry leaves to the hot oil. Fry until charred, switch off the heat and immediately add it to the dal and close the lid for few minutes for the flavour and aroma to get infused into the dal. Serve hot.

*Serves 4*

# Naan Qalia

## INGREDIENTS

- 1½ kg mutton, cut into pieces
- 3 tablespoons oil
- 2 large onions, sliced
- 2 tablespoons ginger-garlic paste
- Salt to taste
- 1 tablespoon turmeric powder
- 1 tablespoon red chilli powder
- 1 tablespoon coriander powder
- 1 tablespoon roasted cumin powder
- 1 tablespoon poppy seeds
- 2 tablespoons desiccated coconut
- 2 cups yogurt
- 1 large onion, finely chopped, browned and made to a paste
- 3 tablespoons bhilawe ki chironji paste
- 4-5 green chillies, slit
- 1 tablespoon homemade garam masala
- Coriander leaves, for garnishing

## METHOD

- Wash the mutton pieces.
- In a cooker, add the oil, mutton pieces, sliced onions, ginger-garlic paste, salt, turmeric powder, red chilli powder, coriander powder and cumin powder. Mutton tends to releases juices so there is no need to add water. If the mutton looks dry, add little water as needed. Cook for 45 minutes to 1 hour on low heat.
- Make a paste of the poppy seeds and desiccated coconut.
- Open the lid of the cooker and check if the mutton is tender. Once tender, add the yogurt, poppy-coconut paste, brown onion paste, chironji paste and green chillies. This will enhance the colour of the qalia and will give an immense flavour to the dish. Cook till it is of a gravy-like consistency.
- Add the garam masala and mix. Garnish with coriander leaves.
- Serve with naan.

*Serves 4*

---

Homemade Garam Masala: Grind together 1 green cardamom, 2 black cardamoms, 1 tablespoon shahi jeera, 3 cloves, 1 tablespoon peppercorns, 2 inches cinnamon, 1 bay leaf, 1 small nutmeg and 1 small star anise to a fine powder.

# Hyderabadi Khatta Murg

## INGREDIENTS

1 cup ghee
3 tablespoons ginger-garlic paste
Whole garam masala (6 cloves, 1 inch cinnamon, 1 mace, 6-7 green cardamoms)
1 kg chicken, curry cut
Salt to taste
½ cup yogurt
¾ cup brown onion paste
½ cup cashew nut paste
½ teaspoon turmeric powder
½ cup tomato purée
1½ teaspoons coriander powder
1 teaspoon red chilli powder
1 teaspoon garam masala powder
½ teaspoon cardamom powder
½ teaspoon mace powder
1 teaspoon kewra water
2½ teaspoon lemon juice
4 tablespoons cream
4 boiled eggs, halved
2 medium tomatoes, cut into wedges
1 teaspoon julienne ginger
1 tablespoon butter
Coriander leaves, for garnishing

## METHOD

- Heat the ghee in a pan, add the ginger-garlic paste along with whole garam masala and sauté. Add the chicken pieces and salt and fry.
- Add the yogurt, brown onion paste, cashew nut paste, turmeric powder, tomato purée, coriander powder, red chilli powder and cook well.
- Add a little water and cover the pan with foil and place it on dum with live coals under the pan and over the lid, till the chicken is well cooked.
- Add the garam masala powder, cardamom powder, mace powder, kewra water, lemon juice and cream.
- Heat the butter on low heat, toss the eggs, tomatoes and ginger in butter and garnish on dish with coriander leaves.

*Serves 4*

# Haleem

## INGREDIENTS

| | |
|---|---|
| ⅓ cup wheat grains, soaked overnight | 2 tablespoons ginger-garlic paste |
| 300 grams mutton, on the bone cut into pieces | 1½ tablespoons skinless split Bengal gram (chana dal) |
| 5 green chillies | 2 tablespoons oil |
| 4-6 mint leaves | 2 tablespoons ghee |
| Salt to taste | ¼ cup yogurt |
| 2 teaspoons coriander powder | 2 lime wedges |
| 2 teaspoons red chilli powder | ⅓ cup browned sliced onions |
| ½ teaspoon turmeric powder | |

## METHOD

- Gently pound the soaked wheat to remove the husk.
- Slice the mutton, add half the quantities of the green chillies, mint, salt, coriander powder, red chilli powder and turmeric powder.
- Add ginger-garlic paste, split Bengal gram, wheat, and oil and boil with sufficient water to cover and cook the meat. Grind to a paste.
- Heat the ghee, add the paste, yogurt, remaining mint, coriander powder, turmeric powder, and salt and simmer. Sauté till the ghee leaves the sides of the pan.
- Garnish with browned onions and lemon wedges.
- Serve hot with sheermals (Hyderabadi bread).

*Serves 4*

# Shahjahani Murgh

## INGREDIENTS

- 2 tablespoons oil
- 3 cardamoms
- 3 cloves
- 1 inch cinnamon
- 2 large onions, finely sliced
- 1 inch ginger, finely chopped
- 12 garlic cloves, finely chopped
- 10 green chillies, finely chopped
- 1 large tomato, finely chopped
- 2 teaspoons coriander powder
- ½ teaspoon red chilli powder
- ½ teaspoon turmeric powder
- Salt to taste
- 1 whole chicken, cut into 8 pieces
- 1 large capsicum, finely sliced
- 1 bunch coriander leaves, finely chopped

## METHOD

- Heat the oil in a kadai, add the cardamoms, cloves and cinnamon. Once they begin spluttering, add the onions and cook till light brown.
- Add the ginger, garlic and green chillies and mix well.
- Add the tomatoes along with the coriander powder, chilli powder, turmeric powder, salt and cook till soft. Add the chicken and mix well.
- Cover cooked till the chicken releases water. Remove the lid and cook the chicken till it releases oil.
- Add the capsicum and cook on low heat till it is soft. Adjust the seasoning and garnish with coriander leaves. Serve hot.

*Serves 4*

# Kabuli Biryani

## INGREDIENTS

1 cup skinless split Bengal gram
3-4 tablespoons oil
1 cup onion, sliced
4 cloves
3 cardamoms
1 inch cinnamon
2 tablespoons ginger-garlic paste
1 tablespoon red chilli powder
1 teaspoon turmeric powder
1 cup yogurt
1 cup coriander leaves, chopped
2 green chillies, finely chopped
1 cup mint leaves, chopped
2 cups Basmati rice, soaked for 30 minutes
3 tablespoons ghee
½ teaspoon saffron strands, soaked in milk
½ cup milk
Wheat dough to seal the pan

## METHOD

❖ Wash and cook the split Bengal gram in 2 cups of water till firm. Heat the oil in a pan, fry the onion till golden brown and set aside on an absorbent paper.

❖ In the same oil, add cloves, cardamoms, cinnamon and the ginger-garlic paste and sauté. Add the red chilli powder, turmeric powder and mix with a little water to avoid burning. Add the yogurt and stir continuously.

❖ Add the cooked gram, half of the chopped coriander, green chillies and mint leaves. Cook until the gravy blends well. Bring 4 cups of water to a boil. Add the rice and cook till three-fourth done.

❖ Grease a heavy bottom pan with 1 tablespoon of ghee, spoon a layer of rice over the bottom. Spoon the dal mixture over the rice. Then layer with some fried onions, chopped coriander and mint leaves, green chillies and cover with more rice. Repeat until all the rice and lentils have been used and then pour 2 tablespoons of ghee over the top. Reserve some onions, mint and coriander for garnishing.

❖ Dissolve the saffron in 3 tablespoons of milk and sprinkle over the rice. Sprinkle the remaining milk as well. Seal the pan with dough and cook on high heat for 15 minutes and then on low heat for approximately 20 minutes.

❖ Garnish with fried onions, coriander and mint leaves.

*Serves 4*

# Lucknowi Biryani

## INGREDIENTS

- 3 cups long grain Basmati rice
- Salt to taste
- 6-8 cloves
- 1½ inches cinnamon
- 4 green cardamoms
- 2-3 mace flakes
- 1 cup green peas
- 100 grams cauliflower florets
- 1 cup carrots, cut into pieces of 1 inch length
- 1 cup French beans, cut lengthwise
- 4 tablespoons oil
- 2 cups onions, sliced lengthwise
- 3 tablespoons ginger-garlic paste
- 6-7 green chillies, slit lengthwise
- ½ cup fresh coriander, finely chopped + as required
- ½ cup fresh mint leaves, finely chopped + as required
- 1 cup yogurt, whisked
- 1 teaspoon turmeric powder
- 2 teaspoons red chilli powder
- A few saffron strands, soaked in ½ cup warm milk
- ½ cup pure ghee
- 1 tablespoon kewra water

## METHOD

❖ Soak the rice in water for 30 minutes.

❖ In a large pan, heat 2 litres of water and season it with 1 teaspoon of salt.

❖ Add the cloves, cinnamon, green cardamoms and mace flakes. Add the rice and allow it to cook on medium heat till three-fourth done. Strain the rice and spread on a large plate.

❖ Boil 2 cups of water in a pan. Add the green peas, cauliflower florets, carrots and French beans. Cook for 5 minutes, drain the water and set aside.

❖ Heat the oil in a handi, add the sliced onions and fry until it turns golden brown. Add the garlic-ginger paste sauté for 1 minute. Add the green chillies, coriander leaves and mint leaves. Sauté for 30 seconds.

❖ Add the yogurt and allow it to simmer on low heat for 1 minute. Add the turmeric powder, red chilli powder, salt to taste and sauté for 1-2 minutes.

- Add the steamed vegetables to the masala. Sauté for 2-3 minutes and turn off the heat.
- Place a heavy bottom pot on heat. Remove half of the cooked vegetables from the pan. Spread half of the cooked rice on top of vegetable layer. Spread the rice evenly. Add some mint leaves, some chopped coriander leaves. Pour some saffron infused milk. Pour some ghee. This completes the first layer.
- For second layer, spread the remaining vegetables and the remaining rice. Add some mint leaves, some chopped coriander leaves. Pour some ghee and some saffron infused milk. Add the screw pine water (kewra water). This completes the second and final layer.
- Cover the edges of lid with dough. Seal the pot and place it on high heat for 15 minutes. Reduce the heat and cook for 20 minutes or till done.
- Serve hot with aloo-pudina raita or vegetable raita.

*Serves 6*

# Kacche Gosht ki Biryani

## INGREDIENTS

½ cup oil
3 onions, finely chopped
2 tablespoons ginger-garlic paste
1 teaspoon garam masala powder
1 teaspoon cardamom powder
1 tablespoon red chilli powder
½ tablespoon turmeric powder
1 kg lamb with bones
1 cup yogurt, beaten
Salt to taste
1 kg Basmati rice
Whole garam masala (4 green cardamoms, 4 cloves, 1 bay leaf, 6-7 peppercorns, 1 inch cinnamon)
½ cup pure ghee
½ cup fresh coriander leaves
½ cup fresh mint leaves
4-5 green chillies, cut into slits
8-10 strands saffron, soaked in 2 tablespoons warm milk
½ cup lemon juice

## METHOD

- In a thick bottom pan, heat the oil and fry half the onions till golden brown.
- Add the ginger-garlic paste, garam masala powder, cardamom powder, red chilli powder, turmeric powder, and meat pieces. Fry for few minutes. Add the yogurt and fry for another couple of minutes. Add 2-3 cups of water and cook till meat is done.
- In another pan, heat approximately 10 cups of water. Add the whole spices and salt. Bring to a boil. Add the washed rice and cook till rice is three-fourth done. Drain the water and remove the rice from the pan.
- To assemble the biryani, take a deep heavy bottom pan and layer the biryani by adding ½ cup of ghee, over it add half of rice. Add a layer of cooked meat masala, using all of it. Then add the coriander leaves, mint leaves, green chillies, milk infused with saffron, lemon juice and fried onion.
- Cover the pan with tight lid and cook on low heat for 20 minutes or till done.
- Serve with raita.

*Serves 4*

---

Note: This is a Hyderabadi biryani.

# Zaafrani Sheermal

## INGREDIENTS

| | |
|---|---|
| A few strands of saffron | ½ teaspoon salt |
| ½ cup milk | Pinch of cardamom powder |
| 1 teaspoon yeast | ¼ cup ghee |
| 1 teaspoon sugar | A drop of kewra essence |
| ½ cup refined flour | A drop of rose water |

## METHOD

- Heat the saffron on a dry tawa or flat pan. Add it to little milk and set aside.
- Soak the yeast in milk with a pinch of sugar to activate it.
- Place the refined flour, salt, sugar, cardamom powder in a mixing bowl. Make a well in the centre and gradually mix in the ghee and activated milk along with kewra essence and rose water. Knead well. Divide the dough into smaller equal portions. Roll these into small flat balls about 4-inches in diameter.
- Lightly brush each with a little ghee or oil. Cook these in the tandoor on in preheated oven at 150°C-200°C for 5-10 minutes till brown, flip and roast the other side.
- Remove and baste with saffron flavoured milk. Wrap in damp napkin and serve with korma, or kebabs.

*Serves 4*

# Taftan

## INGREDIENTS

1 cup warm milk
1 tablespoons sugar
2 teaspoons yeast
3 cups flour
½ teaspoon salt
2 tablespoons yogurt
1 egg, beaten
2 tablespoons oil
2 tablespoons ghee
1 tablespoon onion seeds or poppy seeds or nigella seeds

## METHOD

- To the warm milk, add the sugar and yeast and set aside to activate (it should become frothy).
- Sift the flour with salt in a bowl make a well in the centre. Add the activated yeast mixture, yogurt, egg and oil. Knead the dough into a smooth and elastic consistency. Place in a greased bowl and keep in a warm place for 2 hours.
- Punch the dough and roll into medium size balls. Brush with oil and set aside to sit for 20 minutes. With a rolling pin, roll out each dough ball in a way that it is broad at one end and very narrow at the other.
- Then pull the narrow end in a way that it is shaped like a tear drop. Brush with ghee, sprinkle and onion seeds and bake in hot tandoor. Remove and apply ghee. Serve hot.

*Serves 4*

# Sewai ka Muzzafar

## INGREDIENTS

- 100 grams vermicelli
- Ghee for frying
- 1 cup milk
- 1 cup sugar
- ½ cup khoya
- 5-6 small cardamoms, ground to a fine powder
- 1 teaspoon kewra water
- Strands of saffron, for garnishing
- 1½ teaspoons raisins, for garnishing
- 1 silver leaf, for garnishing
- ½ teaspoon sliced pistachio, for garnishing

## METHOD

- Fry the vermicelli in ghee and set aside.
- Heat the milk in a pan, add the sugar and a little water, simmer and reduce the milk to a single strand consistency.
- Add the fried vermicelli.
- Heat the ghee, add the khoya and raisins and cook till the khoya turns brown. Sprinkle it over the vermicelli mixture. Cook covered on moderate heat till well done. Remove the lid and add the powdered cardamom, kewra water and mix well.
- Garnish with the saffron, raisins, silver leaf and pistachios.

*Serves 4*

# Badam ki Jali

## INGREDIENTS

2 cups almonds, soaked overnight and skinned

6 tablespoons milk

3½ cups sugar

½ tablespoon cardamom powder

1 sheet silver leaf

## METHOD

- Grind the soaked almonds with milk to make a smooth paste.
- In a saucepan, add 1 cup of water and 2 cups of sugar and cook on medium heat.
- Add the cardamom powder and cook till it becomes a syrup of a thin consistency.
- Mix the almond paste into the syrup gently and continue to cook on medium heat till the mixture leaves the sides of the pan and comes to a boil. Take the pan off the heat and allow the mixture to cool down slightly.
- Roll the mixture into lime sized balls.
- Grind the remaining sugar to a powder and dust a circular rolling board with it. Roll half of the balls into flat 2-inch discs.
- Place them on a greased baking tray and moisten the sides by dipping your finger into a bowl of water and tracing the sides.
- Cut out pieces of the silver leaf and cover each disc with it.
- Roll out the rest of the balls into 2-inch round discs.
- Use a round cutter to create a design.
- Lay each one on the varaq covered disc on the baking tray to dry. Serve.

*Serves 6*

# ROYAL Flavours

# Ratalu Rajwadi

INGREDIENTS

- ½ kg yam (ratalu), cut into thick round pieces
- ½ cup ghee
- Salt to taste
- 1 teaspoon red chilli powder
- 1 teaspoon coriander powder
- ½ teaspoon cumin seeds
- 1 teaspoon turmeric powder
- ½ cup onion paste
- 1 tablespoon garlic paste

METHOD

- Prick the yam pieces well with a fork.
- Heat the ghee in a pan and add all the ingredients except the yam.
- Cook till brown and cook till the ghee separates from the masala.
- Add the yam and let it cook. Add approximately 2 cups of water and cook on low heat till the yam is tender and the water dries up completely.
- Infuse the yam with charcoal smoke (dhungar) and serve.

*Serves 4*

# Goolar Kebab

## INGREDIENTS

½ kg wild figs (anjeer/goolar)

½ cup skinless split Bengal gram (chana dal)

Salt to taste

1 tablespoon red chilli powder

A pinch of cumin seeds

1 teaspoon turmeric powder

1 teaspoon garlic paste

1 tablespoon vinegar

1 pinch garam masala

1 medium onion, finely chopped

A little ghee for frying

## METHOD

- Wash and cut each fig into 4 pieces. Soak them completely in water for 2 hours so that they are clean.
- Boil 1 cup of water in a pan; add the fig pieces along with the split Bengal gram, salt, red chilli powder, cumin seeds, turmeric powder, garlic paste and vinegar.
- Cook till the mixture is done and the water dries up completely.
- Add the garam masala and grind the mixture to a fine paste. Divide the paste into 24 equal parts.
- Flatten each ball, place some chopped onion in the centre and shape them into round kebabs.
- Fry them in very little ghee on low heat. Serve with chutney.

*Serves 4*

# Jaisalmer Channa

## INGREDIENTS

1 cup black Bengal gram (kaala channa), soaked overnight

Salt to taste

2-3 teaspoons mustard oil

3 bay leaves

2 inches cinnamon

1 teaspoon cumin seeds

2 mathania chillies

2 teaspoons garlic paste

1 teaspoon ginger paste

1 teaspoon yogurt

1 teaspoon red chilli powder

½ teaspoon turmeric powder

1 teaspoon cumin powder

1 teaspoon coriander powder

2 tablespoons gram flour

Coriander leaves, for garnishing

### For the tempering

2 tablespoons ghee

1 teaspoon mustard seeds

Pinch of asafoetida

3 mathania chillies

## METHOD

- Soak the black Bengal gram overnight. Wash and boil with pinch of salt.
- Reserve ½ cup of the gram and mash the rest of it.
- Heat the oil in a kadai and add the bay leaf, cinnamon and cumin seeds. Allow them to splutter. Add the mathania chillies and mix. Mix the ginger paste and garlic paste with a little water. Add it to the gravy and cook.
- To the yogurt, add the chilli powder, turmeric powder, salt, cumin powder, coriander powder and gram flour. Add this mixture to the kadai. Add little water and cook. The consistency should be thick.
- Add the mashed gram and mix well. Add water if required. Add the gram that was set aside and cook till the oil separates.
- For the tempering, heat the ghee in a pan and add the other ingredients. Pour over the gravy. Mix well. Garnish with coriander leaves.

*Serves 4*

# Pithod Masala

### INGREDIENTS

1 cup gram flour
½ cup yogurt
1 tablespoon oil
½ teaspoon asafoetida
½ teaspoon cumin seeds
Salt to taste
½ teaspoon red chilli powder
½ teaspoon fennel seeds
Oil for deep-frying
Coriander leaves, for garnishing

For the gravy

4 tablespoons oil
3-4 whole dried red chillies
1 cup onion, finely chopped
1 teaspoon ginger paste
1 teaspoon garlic paste
2 teaspoons coriander powder
½ teaspoon turmeric powder
2 teaspoons Kashmiri red chilli powder
½ teaspoon garam masala powder
Salt to taste
1½ cups yogurt
1 tablespoon gram flour
1 tablespoon lemon juice

### METHOD

- For the pithod, mix the gram flour, yogurt, oil, asafoetida, cumin seeds, salt, red chilli powder and fennel seeds in a bowl.
- Add the water and mix to ensure no lumps are formed. Transfer the batter to a non-stick pan and cook till the gram flour becomes thick and leaves the side of the pan.
- Pour the batter on a greased plate and flatten it. Set aside to cool. Cut into square pieces. Heat the oil in a frying pan and deep-fry the pithod.
- For the gravy, heat oil in a pan, add the dried red chillies and fry.
- Add the onions and fry till light brown. Add the ginger-garlic paste, coriander powder, turmeric powder, Kashmiri red chilli powder, garam masala powder and salt with a dash of water to prevent the spices from burning.
- Add the yogurt mixed with the gram flour. Whisk to ensure no lumps are formed. Cook for 1 minute and add 1 cup and bring to a boil till the oil separates. Add the lemon juice and mix. Add the pithod in the gravy and bring it to a boil. Garnish with coriander leaves.

*Serves 4*

# Dal-Baati-Churma

INGREDIENTS

**For the churma**

1 cup coarse wholewheat flour

¼ cup semolina

4 tablespoons melted ghee

Ghee for deep-frying + as required

2 tablespoons almond slivers

¼ teaspoon cardamom powder

5 tablespoons powdered sugar

**For the dal**

5 tablespoons skinless split Bengal gram (chana dal)

5 tablespoons skinless split pigeon peas (toor dal)

5 tablespoons split green gram (green moong dal)

1 tablespoon skinless split black gram (white urad dal)

Salt to taste

3 tablespoons ghee

3 cloves

2 bay leaves

1 teaspoon cumin seeds

2 green chillies, silted

Pinch of asafoetida

1 teaspoon garlic paste

1 cup finely chopped onions

1 cup finely chopped tomatoes

1 teaspoon coriander powder

½ teaspoon turmeric powder

1 tablespoon chilli powder

½ teaspoon garam masala

1 tablespoon finely chopped coriander

**For the baatis**

1 cup coarse wholewheat flour

½ cup semolina

2 tablespoons gram flour

½ cup milk

4 tablespoons melted ghee

1 teaspoon fennel seeds

¼ teaspoon carom seeds

Salt to taste

Ghee for deep-frying

**For the topping**

4 tablespoons melted ghee

8 tablespoons finely chopped onion

2 teaspoons lemon juice

METHOD

- For the churma, combine the wholewheat flour, semolina and melted ghee in a deep bowl and mix well. Add approximately ¼ cup of water and knead well to make stiff dough.
- Divide the dough in to 8 equal portions. Shape each dough portion in the shape of fist and press with your fingers in the centre of each portion to make an indentation.
- Heat the ghee in a deep non-stick kadai and deep-fry a few of the dough portions at a time on a low heat till golden brown from all the sides. These will take a long time to fry as the insides also need to be cooked.
- Drain on absorbent paper and allow them to cool. Break the fry dough balls into a fine powder. Add the almonds, cardamom powder and powdered sugar and mix well. Set aside.
- For the dal, combine the dals with 4 cups of water and salt in a pressure cooker, mix well and cook till the pressure is released thrice (3 whistles).
- Heat the ghee in a deep non-stick kadai add the cloves, bay leaves, cumin seeds, green chillies and asafoetida and sauté on a medium heat for a few seconds.
- When the seeds splutter, add the garlic paste and onion and sauté on a medium heat for 2-3 minutes.
- Add the tomatoes, coriander powder, turmeric powder, chilli powder and garam masala, mix well and cook on a medium heat for 2 minutes, while stirring occasionally.
- Add the cooked dals along with the water, a little salt, mix well and cook on a medium heat for 2-3 minutes, while stirring occasionally. Add the coriander and mix well. Set aside.
- For the baatis, combine all the ingredients in a deep bowl and knead into semi-stiff dough, without using any water.
- Divide the dough into 8 equal portions and shape each portion in a round figure.
- Flatten the rounds; make a small indentation in the centre of the baatis using your thumb. Set aside.
- Boil enough water in a deep non-stick kadai, add all the baatis into the boiling water and cook on a high heat for 15 minutes, while turning them occasionally. Drain and allow them to cool completely.
- Heat the ghee in a deep non-stick kadai, add 4 baatis at a time and deep-fry till golden brown from all the sides. Drain on an absorbent paper and set aside.
- Warm the dal again till piping hot, top it with chopped onion and lemon juice. Serve with the baati and churma.

*Serves 6*

# Jodhpuri Gulab Jamun ki Sabzi

## INGREDIENTS

**For the gulab jamun**

1 cup grated cottage cheese (paneer)

1 cup khoya (mawa), grated

2 tablespoons refined flour

Salt to taste

2 tablespoons oil

**For the gravy**

1 onion, chopped

2 onions, sliced

1 green chilli

1 tomato

Oil, as required

1 teaspoon spice powder (consisting of green cardamom, cinnamon and nutmeg) + as required

1 teaspoon ginger paste

1 teaspoon garlic paste

½ teaspoon turmeric powder

1 teaspoon red chilli powder

1 teaspoon coriander powder

1 cup yogurt

10-12 cashew nuts, soaked and ground to a paste

Salt to taste

2 tablespoons khoya (mawa)

## METHOD

- For the jamuns, in a bowl, add the cottage cheese, khoya, refined flour and salt and knead it till no cracks are seen.
- Shape them into small balls and deep-fry in medium hot oil on low heat till golden brown.
- For the gravy, grind together the chopped onion, green chilli and tomato to make a paste.
- Heat the oil in a pan, add a pinch of spice powder and cook on low heat.
- Add the sliced onions and cook till translucent. Add the ginger paste, garlic paste with a dash of water. Add the turmeric powder, red chilli powder, coriander powder and mix well. Add the onion-tomato paste and cook till the oil separates.
- Add the yogurt and cook till the oil floats on top and stir continuously.
- Add the cashew nut paste and 1 cup of water. Bring to boil. Add the salt, khoya, remaining spice powder and gently add the gulab jamuns. Serve hot.

*Serves 4*

# Sagpaita Dal

## INGREDIENTS

| | |
|---|---|
| ½ cup mixed dal (mix lentils) | ½ teaspoon turmeric powder (optional) |
| 500 grams spinach or bathua or fenugreek leaves (methi) or any other leafy vegetable (saag), washed well and finely chopped | 2 tablespoons ghee<br>1-2 dry red chillies<br>½ tablespoon cumin seeds |
| 8-10 garlic cloves | 1 tomato (optional) |
| 2 pinches of asafoetida | 1 onion, chopped (optional) |
| Salt to taste | ½ tablespoon garam masala (optional) |

## METHOD

- Add the mixed dal, vegetable and 4 cups of water to a pressure cooker.
- Grind together 4 garlic cloves and asafoetida to make a paste.
- Add the garlic paste, salt, turmeric powder and cook in a pressure cooker on high heat till the pressure is released once (1 whistle). Reduce the heat to low and cook for 5 more minutes.
- For the tempering, heat the ghee in a pan, add the red chillies, cumin seeds and the remaining garlic. Fry till the garlic is brown. You can also add the tomato, onion and garam masala. Cook it on high heat for 2-3 minutes (optional).
- Pour the tempering over the dal and garnish with coriander leaves. Serve hot with chapati or rice.

*Serves 4*

# Gondal Chicken

## INGREDIENTS

| | |
|---|---|
| 3 tablespoons oil | 2 whole red chillies |
| 4 bay leaves | 4 tomatoes, pricked with a fork |
| 2 inches cinnamon | Handful of chopped coriander |
| 4 cloves | Salt to taste |
| 6 chillies | ¼ teaspoon turmeric powder |
| 1 teaspoon cumin seeds | 500 grams chicken |

## METHOD

- Heat the oil in a cooker, add the bay leaves, cinnamon, cloves, green chillies, cumin powder, red chillies, tomatoes, chopped coriander, salt, turmeric powder and chicken, mix well.
- Cook in a pressure cooker till the pressure is released three to four times (3-4 whistles), or till done.
- Serve with peas pulao.

*Serves 4*

# Maharaja Chicken

## INGREDIENTS

- 4 tablespoons pure ghee
- 2 onions, sliced
- 1 inch fresh ginger, chopped
- 6 garlic cloves, chopped
- 2 dried red chillies, chopped
- 2 green chillies, chopped
- ¼ cup yogurt
- 1 teaspoon cumin seeds
- 3 teaspoons coriander powder
- 1 teaspoon garam masala
- 1 teaspoon turmeric powder
- ¼ teaspoon ground black pepper
- 2 tablespoons white poppy seeds, ground
- 1 kg chicken, cubed
- 1¼ teaspoons salt
- 2 tablespoons ground almonds
- 1 tablespoon lemon juice
- 2 tablespoons coriander leaves chopped (optional)
- 2 tablespoons pistachios, chopped

## METHOD

- Heat the ghee in a pan on medium heat and fry the onions, ginger, garlic, red chillies and green chillies for 5 minutes. Remove from heat and allow it to cool a little.
- Blend together the yogurt and the cooked onion mixture to make a pureé.
- In the same pan, over medium heat add the cumin seeds, coriander powder, garam masala, turmeric powder, ground black pepper and poppy seeds. Cook for 2 minutes.
- Add the chicken and stir-fry for 5 minutes. Cook covered on low for 20 minutes, stirring every few minutes.
- Add the blended onions paste and ¾ cup of water and salt. Bring to a boil and simmer covered till the chicken is tender. Stir to ensure the sauce does not stick or burn.
- Add the ground almonds, stir and cook uncovered for 3 minutes.
- Stir in the lemon juice and remove the pan from the heat.
- Serve garnished with the coriander leaves and pistachios.

*Serves 4*

# Safed Maas

INGREDIENTS

| | |
|---|---|
| 3 onions, peeled and cubed | 1 tablespoon ginger-garlic paste |
| Salt to taste | 3 tablespoons almond-cashew nut paste |
| 500 grams mutton | 2 tablespoons yogurt |
| 4 tablespoon ghee | ½ cup milk |
| 1 teaspoon cumin seeds | 1 tablespoon cream |
| 2 inches cinnamon | A pinch of nutmeg |
| 2 bay leaves | A pinch of mace powder |
| 5-6 green cardamoms | Coriander leaves, for garnish |

METHOD

- Boil the onions in water for about 10 minutes. Strain the onions and grind to a paste with salt.
- Boil the mutton in water with little salt till half cooked.
- Heat the ghee in a pan, add the cumin seeds, cinnamon, bay leaves and cardamoms. Allow them to splutter.
- Add the onion paste and cook for a minute. Add the ginger-garlic paste and mix well.
- Adjust the seasoning, add the mutton and cook covered till done.
- Add the almond-cashew nut paste, yogurt, milk and cream and mix well. Add the nutmeg powder and mace powder. Mix well and cook for another 10 minutes.
- Garnish with coriander leaves.

*Serves 4*

# Banjara Mutton

## INGREDIENTS

- 2 teaspoons poppy seeds
- 1 inch ginger
- 3 teaspoons roasted channa dal
- 3-4 dried Kashmiri red chillies
- 3 tablespoons grated dry coconut
- 10 garlic cloves
- 4 sprigs of coriander leaves
- 2 onions, chopped
- 1 tablespoon oil
- 2 tomatoes, finely chopped
- ½ cup yogurt
- 1 kg mutton
- Salt to taste
- 2 teaspoons red chilli powder
- ¼ teaspoon cinnamon powder
- 1 bay leaf powder
- 1 teaspoon garam masala
- 1 teaspoon turmeric powder
- Coriander leaves, for garnishing

## METHOD

- Grind together the poppy seeds, ginger and channa dal to make a paste and set aside.
- Grind together the red chillies, coconut, garlic and coriander to make a paste and set aside.
- Fry the onions without oil and allow it to cook till it begins to brown. Then add the oil and begin stirring them.
- Once the onions begin to brown, add the green paste and cook for 5 minutes till it is cooked.
- Add the poppy seed paste and cook further. Add tomatoes and yogurt and mix well. Add the mutton and mix well.
- Add the salt, red chilli powder, cinnamon powder and bay leaf powder and mix well.
- Cook covered till the mutton releases juices and it is tender. Add the garam masala and turmeric powder and cook for another 5 minutes. Garnish with the coriander leaves.

*Serves 6*

# Laal Maas

### INGREDIENTS

- 18-20 dried red chillies
- 2 teaspoons coriander seeds
- 1 teaspoon cumin seeds
- 1 cup mustard oil
- 10 garlic cloves, finely chopped
- ½ teaspoon ginger, finely chopped
- 500 grams mutton, cut into pieces with bones
- Salt to taste
- 1 cup kachri powder (Kachri is a dried vegetable, a variety of cucumbers found in Rajasthan and ground into a powder)
- 2 small onions, finely chopped
- 3-4 small cardamoms
- ½ teaspoon black peppercorns
- 1 inch cinnamon
- A pinch of mace
- 1 black cardamom
- Handful of coriander leaves, chopped + as required

### METHOD

- Dry-roast the dried red chillies. Then add the coriander seeds and cumin seeds and dry-roast them as well. Grind together to make a fine powder and set aside.
- Heat the mustard oil in a pan, add the garlic and ginger. Once they turn slightly brown add the mutton pieces and mix well.
- Add the salt and kachri powder. This powder tenderizes the meat and also gives it a tangy flavour. Add the onions, mix and roast. Add the cardamom, black peppercorns, cinnamon, mace and black cardamom. Stir well.
- Add the red chilli powder mix and roast for 1 minute. Add enough water to cook the mutton. Cover it and let it simmer for a couple of minutes till the meat is cooked.
- Take out all the mutton pieces on a platter and strain the gravy to remove the whole spices from it. Add the mutton pieces back into the strained gravy and place it back on low heat.
- Add about ½ cup of water and some coriander leaves. Let it simmer for a while and when the gravy reaches a good consistency, take it off the heat.
- Serve hot with a good garnishing of chopped coriander leaves.

*Serves 4*

ROYAL FLAVOURS

# Jodhpuri Kabuli Rice

## INGREDIENTS

1 cup cauliflower florets

1 medium potato, peeled and cut into thin slices

3-4 bread slices, cut into small cubes

Ghee for deep-frying

½ cup green peas, boiled

10-12 cashew nuts

15-20 raisins

Coriander leaves, for garnishing

¼ cup pomegranate seeds

Fried onions, for garnishing

### For the rice

2 cups long grain Basmati rice, soaked for 30 minutes and drained

2 teaspoons lemon juice

2 teaspoons salt

2-3 cloves

A pinch of yellow food colour

### For the masala

2 tablespoons ghee

2-3 cloves

5-6 cardamoms

½ teaspoon caraway seeds (shahi jeera)

½ teaspoon cumin seeds

10-12 black peppercorns

½ cup onions, chopped

1 teaspoon green chilli, chopped

½ cup yogurt

2 tablespoons fresh cream

1 teaspoon coriander powder

½ teaspoon red chilli powder

½ teaspoon white pepper powder

Salt to taste

## METHOD

- Deep-fry the cauliflower florets, potato, bread slices and dried fruits separately, in ghee until golden brown.
- For the rice, in a heavy bottom pan, add the drained rice with lemon juice, salt and cloves and 6 cups water. Boil the rice till three-fourth done. Strain and remove in a colander.
- For the masala, heat the ghee in a pan, add the cloves, cardamoms, caraway seeds, cumin seeds, peppercorns and fry for a few seconds.

- Add the onions and green chilli and fry till the onions turns translucent. Add the yogurt and cream and fry for 2-3 minutes.
- Add the coriander powder, red chilli powder, white pepper powder and salt and cook for 1 minute. Add the fried vegetables, green peas, bread and dried fruits and mix well.
- To layer the rice, transfer half the rice in a heavy bottom pan. Top it up with the masala mixture. Top it with another layer of rice. Sprinkle the yellow food colour.
- Place a tawa on low heat and place the pan with rice on it. Cook for 10-15 minutes on low heat till rice is done. Remove from heat and let it rest for 3-4 minutes. Fluff the rice with a fork.
- Garnish with the coriander leaves, pomegranate seeds and fried onions. Serve hot with raita.

*Serves 6*

# Ram Khichadi

## INGREDIENTS

- 4 tablespoons oil
- 1 teaspoon cumin seeds
- 3-4 cloves
- 1 bay leaf
- 1 inch cinnamon
- 1 onion, chopped
- 1 potato, cut in cubes
- ½ cup green peas, fresh or frozen
- ½ cup green beans, chopped
- 1 cup cauliflower florets
- Salt to taste
- 1 teaspoon turmeric powder
- 1 teaspoon garam masala
- 1 teaspoon red chilli powder
- 1 cup rice, washed and drained
- ½ cup skinless split green gram or split green gram (moong dal), washed and drained
- ¼ cup coriander leaves, chopped

## METHOD

- Heat the oil in a pressure cooker, cumin seeds, cloves, bay leaf and cinnamon.
- When the cumin seeds begin to splutter, add the onion and sauté until lightly brown.
- Add the chopped vegetables and stir. Add the salt, turmeric powder, garam masala, red chilli powder and mix well.
- Add the rice, dal and 4 cups of water. Cook in a pressure cooker till the pressure is released 2-3 times (2-3 whistles).
- Add chopped coriander leaves and serve hot.

*Serves 4*

# Kesariya Metha Chawal

INGREDIENTS

1 cup Basmati rice, soaked for 30 minutes
2-3 cloves
4 green cardamoms
¼ cup ghee
10-12 raisins
5 almonds, shredded
1¼ cups sugar or jaggery
10 saffron strands
Dough to seal the lid of the pan

METHOD

- In a pan, add 4 cups of water, drained rice, cloves and cardamoms and bring to a boil, then lower the heat and simmer (approximately 12 minutes), till the rice is almost cooked.
- Drain the rice in a colander and rinse it twice in cold water. Set aside to drain.
- In a heavy bottom pan, heat the ghee and fry the raisins and the almonds and sauté till they change colour a little. Remove them from the ghee and set aside.
- Add the rice to the same ghee and mix well.
- Grease the edge of the lid and line it with a rolled string of dough along it. Grease the dough a little.
- Lower the heat, remove half the rice and sprinkle half the sugar, and then layer the rest of the rice and the rest of the sugar over it. Add the saffron strands soaked in water or milk. Put the lid on to seal and place the pan over a tawa on low heat for 15 minutes.
- Break the seal and served garnished with the raisins.

*Serves 4*

# Boot ka Halwa

## INGREDIENTS

½ kg fresh green gram (choliya)
¼ cup ghee
½ cup wholewheat flour
2 cups full fat milk
½ cup sugar
1 teaspoon cardamom powder
Cashew nuts, for garnishing
Pistachios, for garnishing

## METHOD

- Boil the green gram in almost 2 cups of water till tender and all the water dries up.
- Grind the gram very finely.
- Heat the ghee in a kadai, add the wholewheat flour and fry till golden. Add the ground gram and cook on low heat, stirring continuously.
- When the mixture stops sticking at the bottom of the kadai, add the milk and stir. When the milk dries up, add the sugar and cardamom powder.
- When it becomes thick and leaves the sides of the kadai, remove from the heat and serve. Garnish with cashew nuts and pistachios.

*Serves 4*

# MAHARASHTRIAN

## Flavours

# Solkadi

## INGREDIENTS

- 10-15 kokum rinds, boiled in 1 cup of water
- ½ grated coconut
- 1 green chilli
- 1 garlic clove
- ½ teaspoon black salt
- ½ teaspoon roasted cumin powder
- ½ teaspoon sugar
- Salt to taste
- Chopped coriander, for garnishing

## METHOD

- Boil the kokum rinds in 1 cup of water. Cool, strain and make a pulp.
- Add ½ cup of warm water and the grated coconut in a grinder along with green chilli and garlic clove and grind to make a milk.
- To the coconut milk add the kokum pulp, black salt, roasted cumin powder, sugar and a pinch of salt.
- Mix well and stain with muslin cloth, and garnish with chopped coriander.

*Serves 4*

# Misal Pav

## INGREDIENTS

2 tablespoons oil
1 teaspoon ginger paste
1 teaspoon garlic paste
1 cup onion, chopped
1 cup tomato, chopped
¾ cup grated coconut
1 cup potato, boiled and cubes

**For the gravy**

3 tablespoons oil
Salt to taste
1 teaspoon red chilli paste
1 teaspoon garam masala
½ teaspoon turmeric powder
1 teaspoon cumin-coriander powder
½ teaspoon cinnamon-clove powder

**For the usal**

3 tablespoons oil
1 teaspoon garlic paste
1 teaspoon ginger paste
½ teaspoon asafoetida
1½ cups boiled matki (moth), soaked overnight
Salt to taste
½ teaspoon turmeric powder
½ teaspoon cinnamon-clove powder
1 teaspoon goda masala
Juice of 1 lime

**For garnishing**

Chopped onion
Mixed dry farsan
Coriander, chopped

**To serve**

Wedge of lime, to serve
Pav, to serve

## METHOD

- Heat the oil in a pan. Add the ginger paste, garlic paste and onion. Sauté till the onion is translucent.
- Add the tomatoes and grated coconut. Mix well and sauté for a few minutes.
- Once cool, grind the mixture to a paste.
- For the gravy, heat the oil in a pan. Add the ground paste and sauté for about 2 minutes. Now add the salt, red chilli powder, garam masala, turmeric powder, cumin-coriander powder, cinnamon-clove powder and mix it.

- Add 3 cups of water or as per your desired consistency and cook till the mixture starts leaving oil.
- Transfer to a bowl and set it aside.
- For the usal, heat the oil in a pan. Add the garlic paste, ginger paste, and asafoetida. Sauté for 1 minute and add the boiled sprouts and potatoes. Mix well.
- Add the salt, turmeric powder, garam masala, cinnamon-clove powder, goda masala and lime juice and cook it for about 8-10 minutes.
- Transfer to a separate bowl.
- For the misal, add the ready usal to a serving bowl and pour the gravy over it.
- Add the chopped onion and farsan.
- Garnish with chopped coriander. Serve with pav and a wedge of lime.

*Serves 4*

---

Note: You may also use mix sprouts to make usal. The farsan can be substituted with chivda as well.

# Nagpuri Mutton Saoji

## INGREDIENTS

- 3 tablespoons oil
- 2 medium onions, sliced
- 8-10 black peppercorns
- 7-8 dried red chillies
- 1 teaspoon lichen (dagad phool)
- 2-3 black cardamoms
- 2-3 green cardamoms
- 1 teaspoon caraway seeds
- 2 teaspoons coriander seeds
- 3-4 cloves
- 3-4 inches cinnamon
- 3-4 bay leaves
- 1 teaspoon poppy seeds
- ½ cup dry coconut, sliced
- 1 kg mutton, cut into pieces
- 2 tablespoons ginger-garlic paste
- Salt to taste

## METHOD

- Heat the oil in a pressure cooker and sauté the onions till they turn golden brown.
- Take off the heat and drain the excess oil from onions. Grind the onions along with a little water to make a paste.
- In the same oil, sauté the black peppercorns, dried red chillies, dagad phool, black and green cardamoms, caraway seeds, coriander seeds, cloves, cinnamon, bay leaves, poppy seeds and dry coconut. Grind them together with water, as required, to make a fine paste.
- Once again heat the oil in pressure cooker and add the mutton and sauté it on high heat till light brown.
- Add the ginger-garlic paste and fried onion and mix well. Once the mutton is fried, add the ground masala paste. Add the salt and 3-4 cups of water; mix well. Boil and then cover the cooker with the lid.
- Cook the mutton in the pressure cooker till the pressure is released thrice (3 whistles). Serve hot with roti and rice.

*Serves 6*

---

Note: This recipe is a delicious non-vegetarian recipe that has the best combination of Indian spices. Additionally, the dry coconut adds extra thickness to the mutton gravy. This recipe is also very famous for being spicy.

# Patwadi Rassa

## INGREDIENTS

**For the patwadi**

- 1 teaspoon oil
- 1 teaspoon cumin seeds
- 1 teaspoon sesame seeds
- A pinch of asafoetida
- 2 teaspoons red chilli powder
- ½ teaspoon turmeric powder
- 2 teaspoons coriander powder
- 1 cup gram flour
- Salt to taste

**For the rassa**

- 2 tablespoons oil
- 2 onions
- 1 teaspoon poppy seeds
- 1 star anise
- ½ teaspoon cumin seeds
- ½ inch cinnamon
- 4-5 black peppercorns
- 1 bay leaf
- 1 black cardamoms
- 2-3 green cardamoms
- 2 tablespoons dry coconut, grated
- 1 inch ginger
- 8-10 garlic cloves
- 2 tablespoons coriander leaves
- Salt to taste
- 1 tsp red chilli powder
- 1 tablespoon coriander powder
- ¼ teaspoon turmeric powder
- 1 teaspoon cumin powder
- ½ teaspoon garam masala powder
- Chopped coriander leaves, for garnishing

## METHOD

- For the patwadi, heat the oil in a pan, add the cumin seeds, sesame seeds, asafoetida, red chilli powder, turmeric powder and coriander powder.
- Add 2 cups of water and bring to a boil. Add the gram flour and salt, stir well and cook covered for 5 minutes.
- Spread the hot patwadi mixture on a greased plate. Allow it to cool and cut into squares. Set aside. Patwadi is ready.
- For the rassa, heat the oil in pan and sauté the onions until brown.

- Add the poppy seeds, star anise, cumin seeds, cinnamon, black peppercorns, bay leaf, black and green cardamoms. Sauté till slightly brown. Set aside to cool.
- Separately roast the grated coconut and allow it to cool.
- Once cool, add the ginger, garlic cloves and coriander leaves and grind together to make a fine paste. Use water if needed.
- Heat the remaining oil, add the prepared paste and sauté till the oil separates from the masala.
- Add the salt, red chilli powder, coriander powder, turmeric powder, cumin powder, garam masala to the paste and continue to sauté. Add water as required to the gravy and bring to a boil on low heat. Once you achieve the desired consistency, add the patwadi to the gravy.
- Garnish with chopped coriander leaves and serve hot with chapati.

*Serves 4*

# Solapuri Khara Mutton

## INGREDIENTS

4 tablespoons oil
4 onions, thinly sliced
1 inch cinnamon
4 bay leaves
8 dry red chillies
2 black cardamoms
10 green cardamoms
10 cloves
½ teaspoon coriander seeds
½ teaspoon cumin seeds
2 inches ginger, finely chopped
15 garlic cloves, finely chopped
2 teaspoons salt or to taste
1 kg mutton, mixed pieces
A pinch nutmeg, grated
1 tablespoon ghee

## METHOD

- Add the oil to a large vessel. Do not switch on the heat.
- Add the onions, cinnamon, bay leaves, red chillies, black cardamoms, green cardamoms, cloves, coriander seeds, cumin seeds, ginger, garlic and salt. Add the mutton and sprinkle it with the grated nutmeg.
- Add ¼ cup of water. Cook covered on high heat for 10 minutes. Stir, you will see water starting to release from the onions.
- Reduce the heat to low and cover with the lid again. Cook on low heat for 2 hours, stirring after every half an hour. (You can also use pressure cooker to reduce time). Then open the lid and increase the heat to high and add the ghee.
- Cook the mutton till the moisture evaporates and the oil begins leaving the sides of the vessel, stirring occasionally.
- Brown the mutton with the gravy for 5 minutes on high heat while stirring continuously so that it does not stick to the bottom of the vessel and burn. After browning the meat for 5 minutes, add ¾ cup of water.
- When it starts bubbling, lower the heat, and cover. Simmer on the lowest heat for 10 minutes. Serve hot with parathas or rice.

*Serves 6*

---

Tips:

- Chop the onions a day in advance and store them in the refrigerator to save time.
- You can use pressure cooker to reduce the cooking time but slow cooked meat tends to be more flavourful and aromatic.

MAHARASHTRIAN FLAVOURS

# Kolhapuri Tambda Rassa

## INGREDIENTS

- 1 kg mutton/chicken
- 1 tablespoon coriander seeds
- 1 tablespoon cumin seeds
- 2-3 bay leaves
- 1 inch cinnamon
- ½ teaspoon black pepper
- 2 star anise
- 2 black cardamoms
- 6 green cardamoms
- 1 teaspoon fennel seeds
- A pinch of nutmeg
- ½ teaspoon mace
- 8 dry red chillies
- ⅔ cup oil
- 1 cup desiccated coconut, grated
- 1 cup fresh coconut, grated
- 2 tablespoons sesame seeds
- 1 tablespoon poppy seeds
- 2 cups onion, chopped
- 1 tablespoon garlic paste
- 1 tablespoon ginger paste
- ½ tablespoon onion-garlic masala
- 1 tablespoon red chilli powder
- ½ tablespoon turmeric powder
- Salt to taste
- 1 tablespoon fresh coriander leaves

## METHOD

- Wash the mutton, strain the excess water and set aside.
- Roast the coriander seeds, cumin seeds, bay leaves, cinnamon, black pepper, star anise, black and green cardamoms, fennel seeds, nutmeg powder, mace, and dry chillies. Grind to a fine powder.
- Heat 1 tablespoon oil, roast desiccated coconut, fresh coconut, along with sesame and poppy seeds till light brown. Grind to a paste using little water.
- Heat rest of the oil, add the onion and roast till brown, add the ginger-garlic paste to it. Add onion-garlic masala, chilli powder, turmeric powder, and coconut paste to it. Adjust the salt. Cook till oil separates from the masala. Add the mutton pieces and mix well.
- Cover and cook on low heat till the mutton releases its juices. Open and cook on high heat till the water evaporates. Add 1½ tablespoons garam masala and mix well. Add water to the mutton as per gravy needed. Tamda rassa tends to be thin, so almost 6 cups of water can be added. Cover and cook on low heat till the mutton is tender.
- Garnish with coriander and serve with lemon wedges.

*Serves 4*

# Malwani Kombdi Vade

INGREDIENTS

500 grams chicken with bones
1 teaspoon lemon juice
4 teaspoons oil
1 onion, finely chopped
A pinch of asafoetida
Salt to taste
Coriander leaves, for garnishing

For the coconut-onion paste

1 fresh grated coconut
1 onion, sliced
2-4 garlic cloves
1 inch ginger
¼ cup coriander, chopped

For the Malwani masala

1 teaspoon oil
2 teaspoons coriander seeds
1 teaspoon cumin seeds
5 dried red chillies
½ teaspoon black peppercorns
3-4 cloves

| | |
|---|---|
| 1 inch cinnamon | 1 small piece lichen (dagad phool) |
| 3-4 green cardamoms | ¼ teaspoon turmeric powder |
| 1 star anise | ½ teaspoon nutmeg powder |
| 1 mace | ½ teaspoon red chilli powder |

## METHOD

- For the malwani masala, heat the oil in a pan and roast the coriander seeds, cumin seeds, red chillies, black peppercorns, cloves, cinnamon, green cardamoms, star anise, mace and stone flower separately. Grind all the roasted ingredients together to make a fine masala powder.
- Add the turmeric powder, nutmeg powder and red chilli powder to the masala powder and mix well. Malwani masala is ready.
- For the coconut-onion paste, dry-roast the grated coconut little. Grind together all the ingredients with a little water to make smooth paste. Set aside.
- For the chicken marinade, to the chicken add the Malwani masala combined with 1 teaspoon of lemon juice. Set aside the chicken to marinate for 30-40 minutes in a refrigerator.
- Heat the oil in a pan. Add the onion and sauté till translucent. Add a pinch of asafoetida.
- Add the marinated chicken and salt to taste. Cook covered for 6-8 minutes, stirring occasionally.
- Add the coconut-onion paste, mix well and cook for 4-5 minutes, then add 2 cup of hot water. When the curry comes to boil, reduce the heat and let it simmer on low heat for about 8-10 minutes.
- Garnished with coriander leaves and serve hot with Malwani wade, chapati or plain rice.

*Serves 4*

# Malwani Kurli

## INGREDIENTS

500 grams King fish fillets, cut into 1 inch cubes

Salt to taste

A pinch turmeric powder

3 teaspoons ginger-garlic paste

¾ cup grated coconut

1 teaspoon coriander seeds

4 -5 dried red chillies

4 tablespoons oil

1 tablespoon garlic, crushed

1 teaspoon cumin seeds

2 onions, chopped

1 sprig curry leaves

2 kokum rinds

Coriander leaves, for garnishing

## METHOD

- To the fish, add the salt, turmeric powder, ginger-garlic paste and mix gently. Set aside for 15 minutes.
- Roast together the coconut, coriander seeds and red chillies. Grind the roasted mixture with a little water to make a paste.
- Heat the oil in a pan, add crushed garlic, cumin seeds, chopped onions and curry leaves. Cook till they turn light brown. Add the prepared paste and cook. Adjust the water consistency as per needed. Add the kokum rinds and boil for about 10 minutes.
- Add the fish fillets and cook for 15 minutes till firm. Take off the heat and serve garnished with coriander.

*Serves 4*

# Shevgyachi Amti

## INGREDIENTS

½ cup split pigeon peas (toor dal)

2 drumsticks (shevga), cut into 3-inch long pieces

1 teaspoon turmeric powder

2 teaspoons jaggery or sugar

Salt to taste

**For the spice paste**

3-4 Kashmiri red chillies, seeds removed

2 teaspoons coriander seeds

½ cup fresh grated coconut

1 teaspoon tamarind water

**For the tempering**

3 tablespoons oil

4 dried red chillies, preferably round red chillies

1 teaspoon mustard seeds

A pinch of asafoetida

½ teaspoon ginger, peeled and julienned

1 sprig curry leaves

2 tablespoons coriander leaves, chopped

## METHOD

- Wash and soak the split pigeon peas for 1 hour. Cut the drumstick into 3 inch long pieces. Don't peel them, just discard the ends of the drumsticks.
- Drain the split pigeon peas and transfer to a cooker. Add the turmeric powder with about 5 cups of water. Once the cooker creates pressure, lower the heat and cook for 15-20 minutes.
- For the spice paste, toss the red chillies and coriander seeds on medium heat for 2-3 minutes in a dry skillet. Allow it to cool and then grind to a fine powder.
- To the powder, add the coconut and tamarind water and grind to a smooth paste.
- Open the cooker and add the paste to the dal along with the drumsticks, jaggery, salt and allow it to boil for about 15-20 minutes.
- For the tempering, heat the oil in a pan. Add the red chillies, mustard seeds, asafoetida and sauté. Add the ginger and curry leaves and remove from heat.
- Pour the tempering over the dal and adjust the seasoning. Garnish with coriander leaves.

*Serves 4*

# Fonna Kadhi

INGREDIENTS

½ teaspoon coconut oil
½ teaspoon carom seeds
4 tirphal or Schezuan peppers
2 dried red chillies, broken into pieces
½ teaspoon turmeric powder
½ teaspoon red chilli powder
2 cups coconut milk
1 teaspoon salt
6 kokum rinds
Coriander leaves, for garnishing

METHOD

- Heat the oil in a pan, add the carom seeds, Schezuan peppers and red chillies.
- Add the turmeric powder, red chilli powder and coconut milk. Add the salt and kokum rinds and bring the mixture to a boil.
- Garnish with coriander leaves. Serve hot with rice.

*Serves 4*

Note: This curry, which is another version of the famous sol kadhi, can also be consumed at room temperature after a meal to help with digestion.

BENGALI
Flavours

# Begun Bhaja

## INGREDIENTS

2 brinjals, cut into thick round slices
2 teaspoons turmeric powder
1 teaspoon red chilli powder
1 teaspoon salt
1 cup mustard oil

## METHOD

- To the brinjal slices apply some turmeric powder, red chilli powder and salt. Set aside.
- Heat the oil in a pan, once it begins to emit smoke, turn off the heat and allow it to cool.
- Heat the same oil once again.
- Shallow-fry the brinjal slices till they are brown and crisp. Place on an absorbent paper.
- Serve hot.

*Serves 4*

# Mochar Ghonto

## INGREDIENTS

1 whole banana blossom
1 tablespoon ghee
2 green cardamoms
2 cloves
1 inch cinnamon
½ teaspoon cumin seeds
1 dried red chilli
½ teaspoon ginger paste
1 potato, chopped
2 green chillies, cut lengthwise or chopped
¼ cup boiled skinless split Bengal gram (chana dal)
1 teaspoon turmeric powder
¼ teaspoon red chilli powder
¼ teaspoon cumin powder
½ teaspoon sugar
Salt to taste
¼ cup grated coconut
½ teaspoon garam masala powder

## METHOD

- Wash and peel the banana flower. Extract the white flowers inside, remove the bracts till you reach the white yellow flower heart. Apply some mustard oil on your hands while cleaning to prevent itching.
- In the flower you will find a feathery plastic like petal back and a matchstick like stem. Pull and remove both as they are not edible and will taste bitter.
- After cleaning all the flowers, finely chop them and pressure cook them in just little water (about ½ cup) till the pressure is released once (1 whistle). Drain the water.
- Heat the ghee in the pan, add the green cardamoms, cloves, cinnamon and fry till they release an aroma. Add the cumin seeds, red chilli and ginger paste, sauté lightly.
- Lower the heat and add the potato. Cook covered for 10 minutes till the potato are partly done. Remove the lid and add the green chillies, boiled split Bengal gram, banana blossom florets.
- Add the turmeric powder, chilli powder, cumin powder, sugar, salt and mix well. Cook on low heat till the florets turn dark brown. Splash a little water frequently to avoid burning.
- Add half the grated coconut along with garam masala powder, stir and mix well. Garnish with rest of the coconut.

*Serves 4*

# Kolkata-style Chicken Kheema Cutlet

## INGREDIENTS

1 kg chicken, minced
4 teaspoons lemon juice
2 onions, chopped
2 teaspoons ginger, grated
2 teaspoons garlic, grated
2 green chillies
2½ tablespoons meat masala
1 cup coriander leaves
1 teaspoon garam masala powder
Salt to taste
4 egg whites
6 teaspoons corn flour
2 teaspoons black pepper powder
Bread crumbs, as required
½ cup oil

## METHOD

- Drain the excess water from the minced chicken with a strainer.
- To the minced chicken, add the lemon juice, onions, ginger, garlic, green chillies, meat masala, coriander leaves, garam masala powder and salt. Mix well and set aside to marinate for 1 hour.
- In a large bowl, mix together the egg whites, corn flour, salt, a little water, black pepper powder to make a thick batter.
- Shape the chicken mince into cutlets and coat them evenly with the breadcrumbs and then dip the cutlets in the egg white batter and set aside. Refrigerate the cutlets for 8-10 minutes.
- Heat the oil in a pan and deep-fry the cutlets till crispy and brown.
- Serve hot with a chutney or dip.

*Serves 6*

# Kosha Mangsho

## INGREDIENTS

**For the marinade**
½ kg mutton
½ cup hung yogurt
1 teaspoon ginger paste
1 teaspoon garlic paste
1 tablespoon mustard oil

**For the gravy**
2 tablespoons mustard oil
2 bay leaves
2 black cardamoms, crushed slightly
3-4 green cardamoms, crushed slightly
1 inch cinnamon, crushed slightly
2-3 cloves, crushed slightly
3-4 dried red chillies
1 teaspoon sugar
1½ cups onions, thinly sliced
1 teaspoon ginger, chopped
1 teaspoon garlic, chopped
½ cup tomatoes, chopped
2-3 potatoes, peeled and cut into halves
2 teaspoons coriander powder
1 teaspoon turmeric powder
2 teaspoons Kashmiri red chilli powder
1 teaspoon cumin powder
Salt to taste
½ teaspoon garam masala powder
2 tablespoons lemon juice
Coriander leaves, for garnishing

## METHOD

- For the mutton, mix together all the ingredients and set aside to marinate for 3-4 hours.
- Heat the mustard oil in a pressure cooker, add the bay leaf, black cardamoms, green cardamoms, cinnamon, cloves, red chillies and sugar, and fry.
- Add the onions and fry until slightly browned. Add the ginger and garlic and fry until browned. Add the tomatoes and cook for 2 minutes. Add the marinated mutton pieces along with the marinade and fry for 5-6 minutes on high heat.
- Add the coriander powder, turmeric powder, red chilli powder, cumin powder and salt and cook for 2-3 minutes. Add 1 cup of water and pressure cook until the mutton is done. Open the lid of the cooker once the pressure is released completely. To the mutton, add the garam masala powder and lemon juice and mix well.
- Cook for another 3-4 minutes until the gravy thickens slightly. Garnish with fresh coriander. Serve hot with basmati pulao or luchi.

*Serves 4*

# Shorshe Bata Maach

## INGREDIENTS

3 teaspoons black mustard seeds

4 teaspoons yellow mustard seeds

3 green chillies

Salt to taste

½ teaspoon red chilli powder

1½ teaspoons turmeric powder

8 fish fillets (Rui/Katla/Pompano/Tilapia/Carp)

6 tablespoons mustard oil

2 pinches of Nigella seeds

Sugar to taste

## METHOD

- Soak the black and yellow mustard seeds for 1-2 hours.
- Grind together the soaked mustard seeds, 1 green chilli, ½ teaspoon of salt and some water to make a thick paste.
- To a bowl, add 3 teaspoons prepared paste, some salt, red chilli powder and ½ teaspoon turmeric powder, and a little water to make a runny paste. Set aside. Marinate the fish with 1 of teaspoon salt and 1 of teaspoon turmeric powder for 5-10 minutes.
- Heat the oil in a pan. Fry the fish on both sides in the oil.
- Reserve 4 teaspoons of oil in the pan for the gravy and remove the excess.
- Heat the oil, add the Nigella seeds and the remaining green chillies, mustard paste, sauté for 2 minutes. Add ½ cup of hot water, salt and pinch of sugar. Mix well for 1 minute.
- Add the fried fish. Cover the pan and cook for 5 minutes in low heat. You can also add chopped coriander leaves if you like.
- Turn off the heat and let it rest for 2 minutes.
- Serve hot with plain rice.

*Serves 4*

# Daab Chingri

## INGREDIENTS

750 grams prawns

1 large tender coconut, grated

2 tablespoons mustard oil

1 teaspoon panch phoron (mixture of onion seeds, cumin seeds, mustard seeds, fenugreek seeds, fennel seeds)

4 green chillies, chopped

1 medium onion, chopped

3 garlic cloves, chopped

3 tablespoons mustard paste

1½ teaspoons turmeric powder

Salt to taste

20 grams wheat dough

## METHOD

- Peel the prawns.
- Grind the grated coconut to make a paste.
- Heat the oil in a pan and add the panch phoron.
- Add the green chillies, onions and garlic cloves. Transfer to a large bowl.
- To the bowl add the mustard paste, turmeric powder, salt and coconut paste and prawns and mix well.
- Cut the bottom of the coconut shell evenly to make it stand properly inside a pressure cooker.
- Transfer the prawn mixture to the shell and cover the top with wheat dough.
- Add some water to a pressure cooker and place the coconut shell inside. Ensure that the water level is half the height of the coconut shell.
- Cook in a pressure cooker, on medium heat until the pressure is released thrice (3 whistles). Take the cooker off the heat and keep the dish in the cooker for 10 more minutes.
- Serve hot.

*Serves 4*

# Cholar Dal

## INGREDIENTS

- 1 cup skinless split Bengal gram (chana dal)
- ½ teaspoon turmeric powder
- Salt to taste

**For the tempering**

- 3 tablespoons ghee
- ¼ cup fresh coconut, thinly sliced
- 1 teaspoon cumin seeds
- ¼ teaspoon asafoetida
- 4- 5 dried red chillies
- 3-4 cloves
- 1 inch cinnamon
- 2-3 green cardamoms
- 2 bay leaves
- 1 teaspoon grated ginger
- 1 teaspoon chopped green chilli
- 2 tablespoons raisins
- 1 teaspoon sugar

## METHOD

- Add the washed skinless split Bengal gram, 3 cups of water, turmeric powder and salt to a pressure cooker and cook till the dal is mushy.
- For the tempering, heat the ghee in a pan and fry the coconut slices till golden brown. Transfer them to a plate.
- In the same ghee add the cumin seeds and asafoetida and let them crackle for a few seconds.
- Add the red chillies, cloves, cinnamon, green cardamoms and bay leaves. Fry for a few seconds. Add the ginger and green chilli and fry for another few seconds.
- Pour the tempering over the dal.
- Sprinkle the raisins, fried coconut and sugar over the dal, mix well and served hot.

*Serves 4*

# Dry Fruit Sandesh

## INGREDIENTS

2 litres full cream milk
3 tablespoons lemon juice
150 ml maple syrup
¼ teaspoon cardamom powder
1½ tablespoons pistachios
1½ tablespoons almonds

## METHOD

- Heat the milk in a thick-bottomed pan over medium heat, and bring to a boil, stirring occasionally.
- Reduce to low heat and add the lemon juice. Mix well until the milk curdles.
- Drain the curdled milk using a piece of cotton cloth. Let the curdled milk remain in the cloth for 30 minutes. Then mash it and transfer to a bowl.
- Add the maple syrup and mix well.
- Add the mixture to a kadai and cook on medium heat for 5 minutes.
- Add the cardamom powder and mix well. Once cool, cut into squares.
- Garnish with the pistachios and almonds. Serve warm or cold.

*Serves 4*

# Hridoy Horon

## INGREDIENTS

**For the pitha**

2 cups milk

A pinch of salt

2 tablespoons sugar

1 teaspoon cardamom powder

2 tablespoons ghee

2 cups refined flour

1 egg

Oil for deep-frying

**For the sugar syrup**

2 cups sugar

1 teaspoon cardamom powder

1 tablespoon ghee

**For the rabri/malai**

2 cups full fat milk

3 tablespoons sugar

1 green cardamom powder

## METHOD

- For the pitha, to the milk add the salt, 2 tablespoons sugar, cardamom powder, 1 tablespoon ghee and boil.
- Add the flour to the boiling milk and remove from heat. Let it cool.
- Once cool, add the egg. Mix vigorously to make a dough. Set aside covered for 30 minutes.
- Divide the dough into 10-12 portions. Roll each into thin flat bread. Fold the flatbread like a paper fan, and fold in half. Seal inside the closed end with wet fingers, fold the open edges opposite way to make the heart shape and seal with water and cut excess part.
- Prepare sugar syrup with 1 cup of water and 2 cups sugar. Once it reaches a single string consistency add the cardamom powder and ghee to it.
- Heat the oil and deep-fry the pitha on low heat till light brown.
- Soak them in the syrup for almost 3 hours. Remember, the syrup needs to be warm.
- For the rabri, heat milk in a heavy bottom pan, once it starts boiling, lower the heat and cook, stirring continuously till it turns thick.
- After the milk turns thick, add the sugar and cardamom powder to it and cook till the sugar melts. Remove from heat, and allow it to cool. Enjoy with chilled rabri.

*Serves 4*

# Kathi/Misti Goja

INGREDIENTS

| | |
|---|---|
| 1 cup refined flour | 2 tablespoons ghee |
| ½ teaspoon baking powder | Oil for deep-frying |
| A pinch of salt | 1 cup sugar |

METHOD

- In a bowl, sieve the flour, baking powder and salt. Add the ghee and a little water and prepare a smooth and stiff dough. Set aside to rest.
- Cut the dough into 3 parts. Roll out each part into a thick roti. Cut the roti into thin and long strips with a knife.
- In a kadai, heat the oil and fry the gojas on low heat till light brown.
- Make a sugar syrup with the sugar and 1 cup water. It should have a single string consistency.
- Add the fried gojas to the syrup. Remove the gojas for the syrup and mix well so that they are well coated. Let them dry and serve cool.

*Serves 4*

# SOUTHERN
## Flavours

# Nellikai Sadam

## INGREDIENTS

- 2 cups cooked rice
- 1 tablespoon oil + 1 teaspoon oil (preferably, sesame oil)
- 3-4 teaspoons mustard seeds
- 1 teaspoon skinless split Bengal gram (chana dal)
- 2 teaspoons skinless split black gram (urad dal)
- 2 dried red chillies
- Pinch of asafoetida
- 1 green chilli, slit
- ½ inch ginger, finely chopped
- A few curry leaves
- A pinch of turmeric powder
- ¼ cup gooseberry, finely chopped
- Salt to taste

## METHOD

- To the rice, add the sesame seed oil. Spread it out on a plate to cool.
- Heat the oil, add the mustard seeds, when they splutter, add the split Bengal gram, split black gram, red chillies and asafoetida.
- Sauté till the dals turns golden brown, add the green chilli, ginger, curry leaves, turmeric powder and sauté for a few seconds.
- Add the chopped gooseberry, salt and cook till soft.
- Add the cooked rice and mix gently.
- Serve with papads and appams.

*Serves 4*

---

Note: You can also use leftover rice for this dish.

# Vegetable Stew

## INGREDIENTS

- 2-3 tablespoons coconut oil
- 1½ inches cinnamon
- 3 -4 green cardamoms
- 1 teaspoon crushed black peppercorns
- 4-5 cloves
- 1 inch ginger, julienned
- 3-4 garlic cloves, crushed
- 2-3 green chillies, slit
- 1 large onion, sliced
- 12-15 curry leaves
- 2 small carrots, chopped
- 2 potatoes, chopped
- ¾ cup green peas
- 70-80 grams French beans, chopped
- 2½ cups thin coconut milk
- 1 cup thick coconut milk
- Salt to taste

## METHOD

- Heat the oil, add the cinnamon, cardamoms, black peppercorns, cloves and sauté till fragrant.
- Add the ginger, garlic, chillies, sliced onion and curry leaves and sauté till the onion becomes translucent. Do not brown the onion.
- Add the carrots, potatoes, green peas and French beans and stir well.
- Add the thin coconut milk or water and salt. Cook covered till the vegetables are tender.
- Add the thick coconut milk. Stir well and simmer for just half a minute. You can also fry curry leaves in a few tablespoons of oil and pour it over the stew before serving.
- Serve with appam and steamed rice.

*Serves 4*

# Pongal

## INGREDIENTS

1 cup skinless split green gram (moong dal)
1 cup rice
Salt to taste
2 tablespoons ghee
5 cashew nuts
2 teaspoons ginger paste
1 teaspoon cumin seeds
1½ sprigs curry leaves
½ teaspoon black peppercorns
¼ teaspoon turmeric powder
2 pinches of asafoetida

## METHOD

- Dry-roast the split green gram till golden and fragrant. Wash under running water.
- Transfer the rice and green gram to a deep pan and add water to submerge it.
- Bring to a boil and turn off the heat. Add the salt.
- Heat the ghee in a pan, add the cashew nuts and fry till golden brown and take them out of the pan
- Add the ginger paste in the pan and fry for 1-2 minutes. Add the cumin seeds, curry leaves, peppercorns, turmeric powder and asafoetida. Add the dal-rice mixture and stir well for 5 minutes. Continue to simmer for 3-4 minutes on medium heat till done.
- Garnish with cashew nuts. Serve with vada and sambhar.

*Serves 4*

# Chemmeen Moilee

## INGREDIENTS

| | |
|---|---|
| 100 grams prawns (chemmeen) | 1 spring curry leaves |
| 1 tablespoon coconut oil | 1 pinch turmeric powder |
| 1 teaspoon mustard seeds | ½ cup coconut milk |
| 4 onions, chopped | Salt to taste |
| ¼ tablespoon garlic, chopped | ¼ teaspoon lemon juice |
| ¼ teaspoon ginger, thin strips | |

## METHOD

- Shell the prawns and wash them well. Remove the black string from the prawns.
- Heat the oil in a pan and add the mustard seeds. Once they splutter add the onions, garlic, ginger, curry leaves and sauté till light brown.
- Add the prawns with turmeric powder and stir.
- Cook covered for 10 minutes. It takes about 10 minutes for the prawns to cook.
- Open the lid, add the coconut milk and simmer. Add the salt, lime juice and switch off the heat and serve hot.

*Serves 2*

# Prawns Kuzhambu

## INGREDIENTS

- 500 grams prawns
- 3 tablespoons oil
- 2 medium onions, chopped
- Salt to taste
- 2 teaspoons ginger-garlic paste
- 1 teaspoon turmeric powder
- 2 tomatoes, chopped
- 2 tablespoons grated coconut
- 1 tablespoon chilli powder
- 1 teaspoon coriander powder
- ¼ tablespoon mustard seeds
- ¼ teaspoon fenugreek seeds
- 3 dried red chillies
- 1 tablespoon skinless split black gram (urad dal)
- 1 sprig curry leaves
- ½ cup tamarind juice
- 1 tablespoon crushed peppercorns
- ¼ bunch coriander leaves, chopped

## METHOD

- Peel the prawns.
- Heat the 2 tablespoons oil in a pan, add the onions and salt, sauté it for 2 minutes.
- Add the ginger-garlic paste, turmeric powder, tomatoes, grated coconut, chilli powder, and coriander powder. Cook covered for 2 minutes. Set aside to cool.
- Once cool, grind to make a paste.
- Heat the remaining oil in a pan, add the mustard seeds, fenugreek seeds, red chillies, skinless split black gram, curry leaves and prepared onion-tomato paste. Mix and cook covered for 5-6 minutes.
- Add the tamarind juice and water as desired, and mix well. Once it comes to a boil, add the prawns, mix well and cook covered for 2 minutes. Add the peppercorns, coriander leaves, cover with a lid and take off the heat.
- Serve with rice.

*Serves 4*

# Chicken Kori Gassi

## INGREDIENTS

| For the masala paste | For the curry |
|---|---|
| 1 teaspoon coconut oil | 1 tablespoon oil |
| 20 shallots (small onions) | 2 sprigs curry leaves |
| 8 garlic cloves | 1 clove |
| 12 Byadagi chillies | 2 inches cinnamon |
| 1 teaspoon ghee | 750 grams chicken with bones |
| ¼ teaspoon fenugreek seeds | 2 teaspoons rock salt or salt |
| ¾ teaspoon cumin seeds | ½ teaspoon turmeric powder |
| 2 tablespoons coriander seeds | ½ cup water |
| 1 tablespoon black peppercorns | 2 cups thin coconut milk |
| | 10 grams tamarind, soaked in ½ cup water |
| | 2 cups thick coconut milk |

## METHOD

- For the masala paste, heat the coconut oil in a pan and sauté the shallots and garlic for 3-4 minutes on medium heat until the shallots are pink and soft. Remove from pan and set aside.
- Add the Byadagi chillies to the same pan and roast for 30 seconds. Set aside.
- In the same pan add the ghee, fenugreek seeds, cumin seeds, coriander seeds and black peppercorns. Roast for a minute until fragrant. Set aside to cool.
- Grind together the shallot mixture, roasted chillies and roasted spices with 1 cup of water to make a very smooth paste.
- For the curry, heat the oil and add the curry leaves, clove and cinnamon. Add the chicken pieces, rock salt, ground masala paste, turmeric powder and water to a pressure cooker. Cook in a pressure cooker till the pressure is released twice (2 whistles).
- Open the cooker and mix well. Add the thin coconut milk and bring to a boil. Add the tamarind water, and thick milk and switch off the heat. Serve hot with appams.

*Serves 5*